OPPOSING VIEWPOINTS®
IN WORLD HISTORY

THE
COLD WAR

Louise I. Gerdes, *Book Editor*

Bonnie Szumski, *Publisher*
Scott Barbour, *Managing Editor*
Helen Cothran, *Senior Editor*

OPPOSING
VIEWPOINTS®
SERIES

GREENHAVEN
PRESS®

THOMSON
™
GALE

San Diego • Detroit • New York • San Francisco • Cleveland
New Haven, Conn. • Waterville, Maine • London • Munich

LIBRARY OF CONGRESS CATALOGING-IN-PUBLICATION DATA

The Cold War / Louise I. Gerdes, book editor.
   p. cm. — (Opposing viewpoints in world history)
  Includes bibliographical references and index.
  ISBN 0-7377-1699-1 (lib. : alk. paper) — ISBN 0-7377-1700-9 (pbk. : alk. paper)
   1. Cold War—History—Sources. 2. United States—Foreign relations—Soviet Union—Sources. 3. Soviet Union—Foreign relations—United States—Sources. 4. World politics—1945–1989—History—Sources. I. Gerdes, Louise I., 1953– . II. Series.
  D843.C57724 2004
  909.82'5—dc22
                                            2003049498

Printed in the United States of America

✳ **Contents**

tempted to expand its empire worldwide. America's policy of Soviet containment was a justified response to a growing threat.

Chapter 2: Coexistence and Conflict

✵ Foreword

On December 2, 1859, several hundred soldiers gathered at the outskirts of Charles Town, Virginia, to carry out, and provide security for, the execution of a shabbily dressed old man with a beard that hung to his chest. The execution of John Brown quickly became and has remained one of those pivotal historical events that are immersed in controversy. Some of Brown's contemporaries claimed that he was a religious fanatic who deserved to be executed for murder. Others claimed Brown was a heroic and selfless martyr whose execution was a tragedy. Historians have continued to debate which picture of Brown is closest to the truth.

The wildly diverging opinions on Brown arise from fundamental disputes involving slavery and race. In 1859 the United States was becoming increasingly polarized over the issue of slavery. Brown believed in both the necessity of violence to end slavery and in the full political and social equality of the races. This made him part of the radical fringe even in the North. Brown's conviction and execution stemmed from his role in leading twenty-one white and black followers to attack and occupy a federal weapons arsenal in Harpers Ferry, Virginia. Brown had hoped to ignite a large slave uprising. However, the raid begun on October 16, 1859, failed to draw support from local slaves; after less than thirty-six hours, Brown's forces were overrun by federal and local troops. Brown was wounded and captured, and ten of his followers were killed.

Brown's raid—and its intent to arm slaves and foment insurrection—was shocking to the South and much of the North. An editorial in the *Patriot*, an Albany, Georgia, newspaper, stated that Brown was a "notorious old thief and murderer" who deserved to be hanged. Many southerners expressed fears that Brown's actions were part of a broader northern conspiracy against the South—fears that seemed to be confirmed by captured letters documenting Brown's ties with some prominent northern abolitionists, some of whom had provided him with financial support. Such alarms also found confirmation in the pronouncements of some speakers such as writer Henry David Thoreau, who asserted that

Brown had "a perfect right to interfere by force with the slave-holder, in order to rescue the slave." But not all in the North defended Brown's actions. Abraham Lincoln and William Seward, leading politicians of the nascent Republican Party, both denounced Brown's raid. Abolitionists, including William Lloyd Garrison, called Brown's adventure "misguided, wild, and apparently insane." They were afraid Brown had done serious damage to the abolitionist cause.

Today, though all agree that Brown's ideas on racial equality are no longer radical, historical opinion remains divided on just what Brown thought he could accomplish with his raid, or even whether he was fully sane. Historian Russell Banks argues that even today opinions of Brown tend to split along racial lines. African Americans tend to view him as a hero, Banks argues, while whites are more likely to judge him mad. "And it's for the same reason—because he was a white man who was willing to sacrifice his life to liberate Black Americans. The very thing that makes him seem mad to white Americans is what makes him seem heroic to Black Americans."

The controversy over John Brown's life and death remind readers that history is replete with debate and controversy. Not only have major historical developments frequently been marked by fierce debates as they happened, but historians examining the same events in retrospect have often come to opposite conclusions about their causes, effects, and significance. By featuring both contemporaneous and retrospective disputes over historical events in a pro/con format, the Opposing Viewpoints in World History series can help readers gain a deeper understanding of important historical issues, see how historical judgments unfold, and develop critical thinking skills. Each article is preceded by a concise summary of its main ideas and information about the author. An in-depth book introduction and prefaces to each chapter provide background and context. An annotated table of contents and index help readers quickly locate material of interest. Each book also features an extensive bibliography for further research, questions designed to spark discussion and promote close reading and critical thinking, and a chronology of events.

✦ Introduction

"After World War II, leaders of both East and West had divided the world into opposing camps, and both sides accused the other of having designs on the world."

For forty-three years, although no war between the superpowers of the United States and the Soviet Union was ever officially declared, the leaders of the democratic West and the Communist East faced off against each other in what is known as the Cold War. The war was not considered "hot" because neither superpower directly attacked the other. Nevertheless, despite attempts to negotiate during periods of peaceful coexistence and détente, these two nations fought overt and covert battles to expand their influence across the globe.

Cold War scholars have devised two conflicting theories to explain what motivated the superpowers to act as they did during the Cold War. One group of scholars argues that the United States and the Soviet Union, along with China, were primarily interested in protecting and advancing their political systems—that is, democracy and communism, respectively. In other words, these scholars postulate that the Cold War was a battle over ideology. Another camp of scholars contends that the superpowers were mainly acting to protect their homelands from aggressors and to defend their interests abroad. These theorists maintain that the Cold War was fought over national self-interest. These opposing theorists have in large measure determined how people understand the Cold War, a conflict that had been a long time in the making.

A History of Conflict

The conflict between East and West had deep roots. Well before the Cold War, the relationship between the United States and the Soviet Union had been hostile. Although in the early 1920s, shortly after the Communist revolution in Russia, the United States had provided famine relief to the Soviets and American businesses had established commercial ties in the Soviet Union, by the 1930s the relationship had soured. By the time the United States established an official relationship with the new Communist nation in 1933, the oppressive, totalitarian nature of Joseph Stalin's regime presented an obstacle to friendly relations with the West. Americans saw themselves as champions of the free world, and tyrants such as Stalin represented everything the United States opposed. At the same time, the Soviets, who believed that capitalism exploited the masses, saw the United States as the oppressor.

Despite deep-seated mistrust and hostility between the Soviet Union and Western democracies such as the United States, an alliance was forged among them in the 1940s to fight a common enemy, Nazi Germany, which had invaded Russia in June 1941. Although the Allies—as that alliance is called—eventually defeated Germany, the Soviet Union had not been completely satisfied with how its Western Allies had conducted themselves. For example, the Soviets complained that the Allies had taken too long to establish an offensive front on Germany's west flank, leaving the Soviets to handle alone the offensive front on Germany's east flank. Tension between the Soviet Union and the Western Allies continued after the war.

During postwar settlements, the Allies agreed to give control of Eastern Europe—which had been occupied by Germany—to the Soviet Union for its part in helping to defeat Germany. At settlement conferences among the Allies in Tehran (1943), Yalta (February 1945), and Potsdam (July/August 1945), the Soviets agreed to allow the nations of Eastern Europe to choose their own governments in free elections. Stalin agreed to the condition only because he believed that these newly liberated nations would see the Soviet Union as their savior and create their own Communist governments. When they failed to do so, Stalin violated the agreement by wiping out all opposition to communism in these nations and setting up his own governments in Eastern Europe. The Cold War had begun.

During the first years of the Cold War, Soviet and American leaders divided the world into opposing camps, and both sides accused the other of having designs to take over the world. Stalin described a world split into imperialist and capitalist regimes on the one hand and Communist governments on the other. The Soviet Union and the Communist People's Republic of China saw the United States as an imperialist nation, using the resources of emerging nations to increase its own profits. The Soviet Union and China envisioned themselves as crusaders for the working class and the peasants, saving the world from oppression by wealthy capitalists.

U.S. president Harry Truman also spoke of two diametrically opposed systems: one free and the other bent on subjugating struggling nations. The United States and other democratic nations accused the Soviet Union and China of imposing their ideology on emerging nations to increase their power and sphere of influence. Western nations envisioned themselves as the champions of freedom and justice, saving the world for democracy. Whereas many scholars see Cold War conflicts in these same ideological terms, others view these kinds of ideological pronouncements as ultimately deceptive. They argue that despite the superpowers' claims that they were working for the good of the world, what they were really doing was working for their own security and economic advancement.

Two Schools of Thought

Ideological theorists claim that the Soviets and the Americans so believed in the superiority of their respective values and beliefs that they were willing to fight a cold war to protect and advance them. Each nation perceived itself to be in a "do-or-die" struggle between alternative ways of life. According to foreign policy scholar Glenn Chafetz, a leading proponent of the ideology theory:

> Ideology served as the lens through which both sides viewed the world, defined their identities and interests, and justified their actions. U.S. leaders perceived the Soviet Union as threatening not simply because the USSR was powerful but because the entire Soviet enterprise was predicated on implacable hostility to capitalism and dedicated to its ultimate destruction. From the earliest days of the Russian Revolution until the end of the cold war, Moscow viewed the United

States as unalterably hostile. Even when both nations were fighting a common enemy, Nazi Germany, the Soviets were certain that the Americans were determined to destroy the Soviet Union.

Other scholars argue that the United States and the Soviet Union chose actions that would promote national self-interest, not ideology. That is, the nations were not primarily motivated by a desire to defend capitalism or communism but by the wish to strengthen their position in the world. These scholars reason that the highest priority of every nation is not to promote its ideology but to protect and promote its own self-interest. Thus, these theorists claim, the superpowers advanced their sphere of influence throughout the world in order to gain advantages, such as a valuable trading partner or a strategic military ally. Moreover, these scholars argue, the superpowers aligned themselves with allies who could protect their interests against those who threatened them. Historian Mary Hampton, a champion of the national interest theory, explains:

> Had ideology been the sustaining force of the cold war, the stability and predictability of the relationship between the two states would not have emerged. Their mutual respect for spheres of influence, the prudent management of their nuclear relationships, and their consistent policy of checking global expansions without resort to direct confrontation are best explained by an analysis based on interest-motivated behavior. . . . From 1946 to 1990, the relationship between the United States and Soviet Union included both diverging and shared interests, and it was a combination of these interests that governed their conduct during the cold war.

Although the differences between these two interpretations of Cold War motivations are fairly clear, applying the theories to explain actual events during the period is more complicated. For example, even though a nation might claim that it deposed a leader in a Latin American nation because the ruler was despotic, the real reason might be that the Latin American country had some resource such as oil that the invading nation coveted. Conversely, invading nations are always vulnerable to charges that they are acting in self-interest when in reality nations often do become involved in other countries' affairs out of a genuine concern about human rights or other humanitarian issues. Both theories have been used to explain many U.S. and Soviet actions during the Cold War, leading to radically different interpretations of events.

The Battle over Europe

Both theories have been used to explain Soviet and U.S. behavior in Europe. Those who believe the Cold War was primarily an ideological battle claim that aggressive Soviet action to quell democratic movements in the nations of Eastern Europe was motivated by the Soviet belief that capitalism harms the masses whereas communism protects them. Capitalism, the Soviets believed, exploits workers, who take home only a small percentage of companies' profits in the form of wages whereas the owners reap huge financial benefits at the workers' expense. Under socialism, in contrast, workers own the methods of production and therefore take their fair share of the profits. Thus, ideologically, the Soviet Union believed it was protecting the oppressed workers in the nations of Eastern Europe by opposing democratic movements. Indeed, the Soviet Union's belief in socialism as the superior economic system informed all of its foreign policy decisions. According to Chafetz, the Soviets believed that "international relations are a reflection of the class struggle in which socialist countries represent the working class and capitalist countries represent the exploiting class. Socialist internationalism referred to the common class interest of all socialist states; these concerns trumped other interests, at least in the minds of Soviet leaders."

According to those who believe ideology-motivated actions taken during the Cold War, the United States reacted negatively to Soviet actions in Eastern Europe because it disapproved of the Soviet Union's undemocratic treatment of Eastern Europeans, who had the right to choose their own systems of governance. "Moscow's repression of democratic movements in Eastern Europe," Chafetz claims, "conflicted with the promises to permit elections that Stalin made at Yalta and Potsdam." In response to Soviet aggression in Eastern Europe, U.S. leaders publicly denounced Soviet actions and increased U.S. military forces in Western Europe. In June 1961, for example, President John F. Kennedy took a stand against Soviet premier Nikita Khrushchev's attempt to occupy the city of Berlin. Although Berlin was located within the borders of East Germany, a Soviet satellite, after World War II the Allies had agreed that both East and West would occupy the city (dividing it into East and West Berlin) because Berlin had strong ties with the West. Capitalism and democracy, however, appealed to many East Germans, who fled to West Berlin by the thousands. This embarrassed the Soviets and threatened their hold on Eastern Europe. In June 1961 Khrushchev threatened to forcibly take West Berlin under Communist rule. Kennedy responded to this challenge by increasing America's combat forces in West Berlin and using billions of dollars approved by Congress to increase U.S. nuclear and conventional weapons throughout Western Europe. Khrushchev's counterresponse was to divide the city of Berlin with a cement wall, barbed wire, and a column of army tanks that remained until November 1989.

Theorists who subscribe to the position that the superpowers were motivated more by national self-interest disagree with the ideological argument used to interpret such events. Hampton maintains:

> Arguments that seek to explain the cold-war competition in terms of ideology . . . should anticipate that the United States would have supported democratic reform movements and uprisings throughout Eastern Europe in this period, such as those that occurred in East Germany in 1953 and in Poland and Hungary in 1956. In fact, the Soviet Union resolved these crises [repressed the movements] without intervention from the United States or its Western allies.

Indeed, the United States did not intervene with overt military action in Eastern Europe, taking a more cautious approach to maintain the balance of power between the two superpowers. National interest theorists claim that this stance suggests that the United States was more interested in maintaining its interests than promoting its ideology. Whereas ideological motivation causes nations to break rules and take risks in the name of some higher principles, these theorists say, nations protecting their self-interest do not want to "rock the boat"; thus, countries motivated by self-interest play by the rules and take fewer risks. In consequence, while the Soviet Union marched into the nations of Eastern Europe to crush democratic movements, the United States, fearing international disapproval and hoping to avoid war with the Soviets, declined to intervene.

The Third World

According to theorists who believe ideology drove Cold War strategy, the United States and the Soviet Union both became involved in the third world to expand their spheres of influence, but for different reasons. The Soviets, unable to control Europe, sought to spread their ideology and expand their sphere of influence elsewhere. According to Chafetz:

> Stalin and his successors were convinced that the legitimacy of their rule depended on validating Marxist-Leninist predictions of world revolution. The beginning of the nuclear standoff in Europe [between the United States and the Soviet Union] made it apparent that fomenting revolution in the industrialized, democratic states of the West was either impossible or too dangerous. As a result the Soviets turned their efforts to exporting revolution to less developed countries. They tended to view all anti-Western movement throughout Latin America, Asia, Africa, and the Middle East through the single lens of [Communist leader Vladimir] Lenin's theory of imperialism. Thus, despite the diverse motives behind revolutions, coups, and civil wars in China, Laos, Cuba, Vietnam, Congo, Ethiopia, Somalia, Afghanistan, Libya, and elsewhere, [Soviet leaders] Stalin, Nikita S. Khrushchev, and Leonid I. Brezhnev characterized them all in anti-imperialist terms.

U.S. involvement in the third world was more complex. Chafetz writes, "Soviet exploitation of decolonization created a painful dilemma for the United States." Although the United States, which regarded itself as a freed colony, was empathetic toward third world nations seeking self-determination and independence from colonial powers, it also viewed many of the regimes as anti-American. Indeed, the leaders of these third world coups and revolutions were often rebelling against increasing U.S. dominance in world affairs. Moreover, revolutionary leaders, inspired by Communist philosophy and weary of years of oppression at the hands of capitalist, democratic powers, were often attracted to the Soviet economic model. In consequence, the United States found itself in the uncomfortable position of opposing nationalist revolutions in order to contain the spread of communism.

National self-interest theorists disagree with this analysis. The fact that the United States did not support these revolutions, they say, proves that the nation was motivated more by self-interest than ideology. If the ideology theory were true, they contend, the United States would have supported revolutions against colonial oppression. The United States had once been a colony and after independence had become a champion of the principle that nations have the right to choose their own systems of governance. Despite its past, the United States did not support these revolutions. Instead, the United States opposed them in order to gain or maintain political and economic allies. Thus, in the eyes of many, U.S. behavior toward the third world was immoral and hypocritical. These theorists believe that the use of less-than-honorable strategies, such as assassinations and secret agreements with repressive regimes, to prevent the success of these national revolutions stained America's reputation across the globe. Of particular embarrassment were some of the actions taken by the Central Intelligence Agency (CIA).

The Central Intelligence Agency

National self-interest theorists find support for their views when examining CIA actions during the Cold War. Since its creation in 1947, the CIA was used as an instrument to carry out U.S. Cold War strategy, particularly during the 1950s and 1960s. The CIA was initially mandated to gather, evaluate, and disseminate intelligence. However, the vaguely mandated "other functions and duties" beyond its core mission led to the expansion of the CIA's function to include counterespionage and covert action. Some of these activities were invaluable to America's security. Foreign policy scholar Loch K. Johnson explains: "Intelligence-collection activities provided warnings about Soviet missiles in Cuba in 1962. Counterespionage uncovered Soviet agents inside U.S. secret agencies." Johnson adds, however, that the CIA sometimes used tactics that conflicted with traditional American values. The CIA resorted to assassination plots against foreign leaders and spied on its own citizens. The agency engaged in paramilitary operations in Southeast Asia and abandoned the native people who had helped them to imprisonment, torture, and death when the United States pulled out of the region. Even covert acts that were deemed CIA successes, in historian Benjamin Frankel's view, were moral failures: "Its role in toppling the ostensibly democratic, though Marxist, government of Guatemala in 1954 seemed to fly in the face of America's commitment to democracy." The fact that the administrations of several Cold War presidents approved these tactics suggests that national self-interest, not ideology, motivated CIA action during the Cold War.

The Development of Alliances

National self-interest theorists also find support for their point of view in the formation of alliances among the Communist nations of the East and the democratic nations of the West over the course of the Cold War. These alliances were designed to protect common interests. "Each state began mobilizing other states," Hampton explains, "trying to form alliances and balance against the other." To maintain a balance of power, these theorists claim, Western nations created the North Atlantic Treaty Organization (NATO) in 1949. The alliance was created largely to discourage an attack by the Soviet Union on the non-Communist nations of Western Europe. In 1955 the Soviet Union and the Communist nations of Eastern Europe formed their own military alliance to oppose NATO, the Warsaw Pact. Whether these alliances were responsible for keeping the peace, the balance of power was in fact maintained.

National interest theorists maintain that an unlikely alliance between the United States and China further supports their position. A rift between the Soviet Union and China, the world's most powerful Communist powers, would make this alliance possible.

A Rift in the East

Most of the Western world viewed China and the Soviet Union as two versions of the same Communist evil, but in reality, Sino-

Soviet relations, not unlike those between the Soviet Union and the United States, had been historically uneasy. The two nations shared the longest land border in the world, the source of border disputes since the seventeenth century. Moreover, during the Communist revolution in China, the Soviet Union had initially supported Chiang Kai-shek rather than Mao Tse-tung, who ultimately defeated Chiang Kai-shek and became the leader of Communist China. However, to offer the newly Communist China some security against the United States, in 1950 the Soviet Union signed the Treaty of Friendship, Alliance, and Mutual Assistance with Mao.

Despite this alliance, the Soviet Union and China had different ideas about the purpose of communism and the direction it should take. The Soviet Union began to rethink its Cold War strategy, choosing less overtly aggressive means of expanding its sphere of influence to avoid directly antagonizing the United States. China, on the other hand, vigorously opposed this stance, favoring continued aggression toward "imperialist" nations. China even accused the Soviet Union of going soft on capitalism. China's vigorous opposition to Western imperialism drove a wedge between the Soviet Union and China.

The conflicts between China and the Soviet Union escalated as both vied for control of satellite states. During the late 1960s the Soviet invasion of Czechoslovakia and the buildup of forces in the Soviet Far East led China to suspect that the Soviet Union would one day try to invade it. Border clashes along the Ussuri River that separates Manchuria from the Soviet Union peaked in 1969, and for several months China and the Soviet Union teetered on the brink of a nuclear conflict. Fortunately, negotiations between Soviet premier Aleksey Kosygin and Chinese premier Zhou En-lai defused the crisis. Nevertheless, Zhou and Mao began to rethink China's geopolitical strategy. The goal had always been to drive imperialist nations from Asia, but such a strategy had led to a hostile relationship with America, the Soviet Union's enemy.

In fact, this strategy had brought China into conflict with the United States in two of the bloodiest clashes of the Cold War, the Korean and Vietnam Wars. However, when President Richard Nixon showed signs of reducing if not eliminating the American presence in Vietnam, China began to see normalization of relations with the United States as a way of safeguarding its security against the Soviet Union. Since this relationship was forged to enhance China's national security and was created despite ideological differences between the two nations, the alliance between China and the United States supports the claims of self-interest theorists.

The Fall of the Soviet Union

Whereas national self-interest theorists find support for their theory in the development of alliances during the Cold War, ideological theorists find support for their position in the circumstances surrounding the fall of the Soviet Union. When Communist ideology eventually gave way to more democratic ideals in the Soviet Union, the union dissolved and the Cold War came to an end. This change, many argue, can be traced to the efforts of one man, Mikhail Gorbachev. When Gorbachev became leader of the Soviet Union in 1985, he began a political, economic, and social program that radically altered the Soviet government, creating a limited democracy. The nation's political restructuring began with a newly created Congress of People's Deputies, which elected Gorbachev executive president. The new government was not without opposition, and remaining hard-line Communists tried to unseat the new government. The coup failed, however, and shortly thereafter Gorbachev dissolved the Communist Party.

Gorbachev tried to create a new Union—the Commonwealth of Independent States—but, explains Chafetz, "this experiment with limited democracy . . . developed a momentum of its own and became too strong for Gorbachev, or his more hardline opponents within the Communist party, to control." When the commonwealth itself collapsed, the new union dissolved into independent nations. Ideological theorists point to this chain of events as proof that Cold War events were largely driven by ideology. Once the Soviet political system changed, there was no longer an ideological rift between the two nations, and the Cold War ended.

For over four decades the United States and the Soviet Union had tried to expand their influence worldwide and in the process came into countless conflicts with one another. Whereas the Soviet Union pressured the nations of Eastern Europe to become

Communist satellites and supported Communist revolutions in Southeast Asia, the United States forged alliances with democratic nations around the world and defended many emerging nations against communism. While trying to interpret these events, Cold War scholars have become divided into two camps: those who think the Cold War powers were acting to further their own belief systems and those who believe the major powers were simply aiming to protect their interests at home and abroad. Which of these theories best explains each superpower's behavior during the Cold War remains controversial. In *Opposing Viewpoints in World History: The Cold War*, scholars debate other controversies surrounding the Cold War in the following chapters: From Allies to Enemies: The Origins of the Cold War, Coexistence and Conflict, From Détente to the Cold War's End, and Reflections: The Impact of the Cold War. The authors express diverse views about the nature of the Cold War and the efficacy and justness of U.S. and Soviet policies. As ideology and national-interest theorists make clear, evaluating the Cold War is an exceedingly complex enterprise.

CHAPTER 1

From Allies to Enemies: The Origins of the Cold War

⊛ Chapter Preface

Many Americans were familiar with communism prior to the Cold War and even tolerated American intellectuals who believed communism might be superior to capitalism. However, attitudes toward communism changed after World War II, resulting in the "Red Scare," a period of anti-Communist hysteria that left a stain on American history.

Following the 1917 Bolshevik Revolution in Russia, during which Communists seized power, some Americans began to view communism as a solution to what they considered to be the evils of capitalism. Many blamed the severe economic depression of the 1930s on capitalist greed, and Communist ideology gained support as a workable economic alternative. Some also viewed communism as a better alternative to the worldwide spread of fascism. Indeed, support for the Soviet Union increased as a result of its role in helping defeat Hitler and Nazism during World War II.

However, American attitudes toward communism abruptly changed after World War II, when many Americans became convinced that the Soviet Union planned to expand its influence throughout the world. In violation of agreements with its former allies—the United States and Great Britain—the Soviets prevented free elections from occurring in Poland in 1947 and installed a pro-Soviet regime in Czechoslovakia in 1948. Moreover, in 1948 the Soviets supported Communist-leaning insurgencies in Iran, Turkey, and Greece, and helped Mao Tse-tung's Communist forces in China. When the United States failed to intervene to change this course of events, some feared that U.S. foreign policy decisions were being made by Communist sympathizers within the government. This fear of Communist infiltration in government and other American institutions led to one of the most infamous Communist purges of the Red Scare. Republican Senator Joseph McCarthy of Wisconsin, whose name came to symbolize the use of false accusations and smear tactics, led this assault.

McCarthy's career in the Senate was rather unremarkable until he exploited the public's fear of Communist influence within the

23

United States in a speech given at a Women's Republican Club meeting in Wheeling, West Virginia, on February 9, 1950. What made his speech notorious was his claim that he had a list of 205 U.S. State Department employees who were Communists, and he specifically named several, describing their crimes and their relationships with others in government. Some of those he accused lost their jobs, although McCarthy never proved their guilt.

According to historian Margaret Mary Barrett, "McCarthyism was instigated by the fear of Soviet aggression. It was a paranoid reaction to Soviet advances in technology, espionage, and the political conversion of other nations in the postwar period. It was, in essence, a drastic domestic response to growing Soviet power." President Harry S. Truman, who claimed that the United States and the Soviet Union were in binary opposition, fueled this fear. According to historian Barak Cohen, "The president declared that Americans 'must choose between alternative ways of life'—the Soviet way versus the American way. By extension any criticism of American policy amounted to defiance of the United States and support for the Communist enemy." This conception of a U.S.-Soviet rivalry created an unreasonable fear of communism that made possible McCarthy's assault, these commentators claim.

When Republicans took over the White House and Congress in 1953, they named McCarthy chairman of the Committee on Government Operations and its Subcommittee on Investigations. In widely publicized hearings on Communist subversion, McCarthy used his position to make reckless accusations using unidentified informers; careers were ruined on the flimsiest evidence. Eventually, McCarthy's bullying of witnesses turned public opinion against him, and, as McCarthy was now targeting a Republican administration, his methods also came under attack by his Republican colleagues. On December 2, 1954, the Senate voted to censure him, describing his acts as "contrary to senatorial traditions."

Although anti-Communist hysteria may have diminished by the mid-1950s, fear of communism remained, and the Cold War continued for another thirty years. In the following chapter political decision makers during the early years of the conflict and historians looking back on the period examine some of the factors, including anti-Communist sentiment, that gave rise to the Cold War.

Viewpoint 1

"The real peace treaty we now need is between the United States and Russia."

The United States Should Seek Peace with the Soviet Union

Henry A. Wallace

Henry A. Wallace—vice president of the United States under Franklin D. Roosevelt from 1941 to 1945—was replaced in the 1944 election by Harry S. Truman, who became president upon Roosevelt's death in April 1945. Prior to Roosevelt's death, Wallace was appointed secretary of commerce but resigned from the position by presidential request after he attacked the administration's harsh policies toward the Soviet Union in a speech given at Madison Square Garden in New York City, on September 12, 1946. He ran for president as the Progressive candidate in 1948, calling for disarmament and an end to the Cold War.

In the following viewpoint, excerpted from his controversial speech, Wallace argues that war with the Soviet Union would be devastating, particularly in light of atomic weapons; thus the United States should seek peace. Ideological differences between the United States and the Soviet Union should not make war between them inevitable, he maintains. Bullying, he claims, will only provoke Soviet hostility.

Henry A. Wallace, speech at Madison Square Garden, New York, September 12, 1946.

Tonight I want to talk about peace—and how to get peace. Never have the common people of all lands so longed for peace. Yet, never in a time of comparative peace have they feared war so much.

Up till now peace has been negative and unexciting. War has been positive and exciting. Far too often, hatred and fear, intolerance and deceit have had the upper hand over love and confidence, trust and joy. Far too often, the law of nations has been the law of the jungle; and the constructive spiritual forces of the Lord have bowed to the destructive forces of Satan.

The Significance of Peace

During the past year or so, the significance of peace has been increased immeasurably by the atom bomb, guided missiles and airplanes which soon will travel as fast as sound. Make no mistake about it—another war would hurt the United States many times as much as the last war. We cannot rest in the assurance that we invented the atom bomb—and therefore that this agent of destruction will work best for us. He who trusts in the atom bomb will sooner or later perish by the atom bomb—or something worse.

I say this as one who steadfastly backed preparedness throughout the Thirties. We have no use for namby-pamby pacifism. But we must realize that modern inventions have now made peace the most exciting thing in the world—and we should be willing to pay a just price for peace. If modern war can cost us $400 billion, we should be willing and happy to pay much more for peace. But certainly, the cost of peace is to be measured not in dollars but in the hearts and minds of men. . . .

I plead for an America vigorously dedicated to peace—just as I plead for opportunities for the next generation throughout the world to enjoy the abundance which now, more than ever before, is the birthright of man.

The Road to Cooperation

To achieve lasting peace, we must study in detail just how the Russian character was formed—by invasions of Tartars, Mongols, Germans, Poles, Swedes, and French; by the czarist rule based on ignorance, fear and force; by the intervention of the British, French and Americans in Russian affairs from 1919 to 1921; by the geography of the huge Russian land mass situated strategically between Europe and Asia; and by the vitality derived from the rich Russian soil and the strenuous Russian climate. Add to all this the tremendous emotional power which Marxism and Leninism gives to the Russian leaders—and then we can realize that we are reckoning with a force which cannot be handled successfully by a "Get tough with Russia" policy. "Getting tough" never bought anything real and lasting—whether for schoolyard bullies or businessmen or world powers. The tougher we get, the tougher the Russians will get.

Throughout the world there are numerous reactionary elements which had hoped for Axis victory—and now profess great friendship for the United States. Yet, these enemies of yesterday and false friends of today continually try to provoke war between the United States and Russia. They have no real love of the United States. They only long for the day when the United States and Russia will destroy each other.

We must not let our Russian policy be guided or influenced by those inside or outside the United States who want war with Russia. This does not mean appeasement.

We most earnestly want peace with Russia—but we want to be met half way. We want cooperation. And I believe that we can get cooperation once Russia understands that our primary objective is neither saving the British Empire nor purchasing oil in the Near East with the lives of American soldiers. We cannot allow national oil rivalries to force us into war. All of the nations producing oil, whether inside or outside of their own boundaries, must fulfill the provisions of the United Nations Charter and encourage the development of world petroleum reserves so as to make the maximum amount of oil available to all nations of the world on an equitable peaceful basis—and not on the basis of fighting the next war.

For her part, Russia can retain our respect by cooperating with the United Nations in a spirit of open-minded and flexible give-and-take.

The Spheres of Influence

The real peace treaty we now need is between the United States and Russia. On our part, we should recognize that we have no more business in the *political* affairs of Eastern Europe than Russia has in the *political* affairs of Latin America, Western Europe and the United States. We may not like what Russia does in Eastern Europe. Her type of land reform, industrial expropriation, and suppression of basic liberties offends the great majority of the people of the United States. But whether we like it or not the Russians will try to socialize their sphere of influence just as we try to democratize our sphere of influence. This applies also to Germany and Japan. We are striving to democratize Japan and our area of control in Germany, while Russia strives to socialize eastern Germany.

As for Germany, we all must recognize that an equitable settlement, based on a unified German nation, is absolutely essential to any lasting European settlement. This means that Russia must be assured that never again can German industry be converted into military might to be used against her—and Britain, Western Europe and the United States must be certain that Russia's Germany policy will not become a tool of Russian design against Western Europe.

The Russians have no more business in stirring up native communists to political activity in Western Europe, Latin America and the United States than we have in interfering in the politics of Eastern Europe and Russia. We know what Russia is up to in Eastern Europe, for example, and Russia knows what we are up to. We cannot permit the door to be closed against our trade in Eastern Europe any more than we can in China. But at the same time we have to recognize that the Balkans are closer to Russia than to us—and that Russia cannot permit either England or the United States to dominate the politics of that area.

China is a special case and although she holds the longest frontier in the world with Russia, the interests of world peace demand that China remain free from any sphere of influence, either politically or economically. We insist that the door to trade and economic development opportunities be left wide open in China as in all the world. However, the open door to trade and opportunities for economic development in China are meaningless unless there is a unified and peaceful China—built on the cooperation of the various groups in that country and based on a hands-off policy of the outside powers. We are still arming to the hilt. Our excessive expenses for military purposes are the chief cause for our unbalanced budget. If taxes are to be lightened we must have the basis of a real peace with Russia—a peace that cannot be broken by extremist propagandists. We do not want our course determined for us by master minds operating out of London, Moscow or Nanking.[1]

A Friendly Competition

Russian ideas of social-economic justice are going to govern nearly a third of the world. Our ideas of free enterprise democracy will govern much of the rest. The two ideas will endeavor to prove which can deliver the most satisfaction to the common man in their respective areas of political dominance. But by mutual agreement, this competition should be put on a friendly basis and the Russians should stop conniving against us in certain areas of the world just as we should stop scheming against them in other parts of the world. Let the results of the two systems speak for themselves.

Meanwhile, the Russians should stop teaching that their form of communism must, by force if necessary, ultimately triumph over democratic capitalism—while we should close our ears to those among us who would have us believe that Russian communism and our free enterprise system cannot live, one with another, in a profitable and productive peace.

Under friendly peaceful competition the Russian world and the American world will gradually become more alike. The Russians will be forced to grant more and more of the personal freedoms; and we shall become more and more absorbed with the problems of social-economic justice.

Russia must be convinced that we are not planning for war against her and we must be certain that Russia is not carrying on territorial expansion or world domination through native communists faithfully following every twist and turn in the Moscow party line. But in this competition, we must insist on an open door for trade throughout the world. There will always be an ideological conflict—but that is no reason why diplomats cannot work out a basis for both systems to live safely in the world side by side. . . .

---

1. In 1946, Nanking, also known as Nanjing, was an important city to the evolving democratic Chinese government led by Chiang Kai-shek.

Speaking Out for Peace

In the United States an informed public opinion will be all-powerful. Our people are peace-minded. But they often express themselves too late—for events today move much faster than public opinion. The people here, as everywhere in the world, must be convinced that another war is not inevitable. And through mass meetings such as this, and through persistent pamphleteering, the people can be organized for peace—even though a large segment of our press is propagandizing our people for war in the hope of scaring Russia. And we who look on this war-with-Russia talk as criminal foolishness must carry our message direct to the people—even though we may be called communists because we dare to speak out.

I believe that peace—the kind of peace I have outlined tonight—is the basic issue, both in the Congressional campaign this fall and right on through the Presidential election in 1948. How we meet this issue will determine whether we live not in "one world" or "two worlds"—but whether we live at all.

Viewpoint 2

"The United States should maintain military forces powerful enough to restrain the Soviet Union and to confine Soviet influence to its present area."

The United States Should Not Seek Peace with the Soviet Union

Clark M. Clifford

Clark M. Clifford played a vital role in the formulation and implementation of U.S. foreign policy during the Cold War while serving as an adviser to Presidents Harry S. Truman, John F. Kennedy, and Lyndon B. Johnson. In 1946 Truman asked Clifford to prepare a secret report outlining relations between the United States and the Soviet Union. In the following viewpoint, excerpted from that report, Clifford—having consulted the secretary of state, the attorney general, and the Joint Chiefs of Staff—claims that Soviet threats and aggression argue against appeasement of the Soviet Union. Clifford argues that the United States should deter further Soviet aggression by increasing U.S. military strength—including atomic and biological weapons—and providing economic support to struggling dem-

Clark M. Clifford, report to Harry S. Truman, 1946.

ocratic nations. Truman implemented many of Clifford's recommendations, including his economic strategy, which came to be known as the Truman Doctrine.

The primary objective of United States policy toward the Soviet Union is to convince Soviet leaders that it is in their interest to participate in a system of world cooperation, that there are no fundamental causes for war between our two nations, and that the security and prosperity of the Soviet Union, and that of the rest of the world as well, is being jeopardized by aggressive militaristic imperialism such as that in which the Soviet Union is now engaged.

An Inevitable Conflict

However, these same leaders with whom we hope to achieve an understanding on the principles of international peace appear to believe that a war with the United States and the other leading capitalistic nations is inevitable. They are increasing their military power and the sphere of Soviet influence in preparation for the "inevitable" conflict, and they are trying to weaken and subvert their potential opponents by every means at their disposal. So long as these men adhere to these beliefs, it is highly dangerous to conclude that hope of international peace lies only in "accord," "mutual understanding," or "solidarity" with the Soviet Union.

Adoption of such a policy would impel the United States to make sacrifices for the sake of Soviet-U.S. relations, which would only have the effect of raising Soviet hopes and increasing Soviet demands, and to ignore alternative lines of policy, which might be much more compatible with our own national and international interests.

The Soviet Government will never be easy to "get along with." The American people must accustom themselves to this thought, not as a cause for despair, but as a fact to be faced objectively and courageously. If we find it impossible to enlist Soviet cooperation in the solution of world problems, we should be prepared to join with the British and other Western countries in an attempt to build up a world of our own which will pursue its own objectives and will recognize the Soviet orbit as a distinct entity with which conflict is not predestined but with which we cannot pursue common aims.

Preventing Soviet Expansion

As long as the Soviet Government maintains its present foreign policy, based upon the theory of an ultimate struggle between Communism and Capitalism, the United States must assume that the U.S.S.R. might fight at any time for the twofold purpose of expanding the territory under communist control and weakening its potential capitalist opponents. The Soviet Union was able to flow into the political vacuum of the Balkans, Eastern Europe, the Near East, Manchuria and Korea because no other nation was both willing and able to prevent it. Soviet leaders were encouraged by easy success and they are now preparing to take over new areas in the same way. The Soviet Union, as Stalin euphemistically phrased it, is preparing "for any eventuality."

Unless the United States is willing to sacrifice its future security for the sake of "accord" with the U.S.S.R. now, this government must, as a first step toward world stabilization, seek to prevent additional Soviet aggression. The greater the area controlled by the Soviet Union, the greater the military requirements of this country will be. Our present military plans are based on the assumption that, for the next few years at least, Western Europe, the Middle East, China and Japan will remain outside the Soviet sphere. If the Soviet Union acquires control of one or more of these areas, the military forces required to hold in check those of the U.S.S.R. and prevent still further acquisitions will be substantially enlarged. That will also be true if any of the naval and air bases in the Atlantic and Pacific, upon which our present plans rest, are given up. This government should be prepared, while scrupulously avoiding any act which would be an excuse for the Soviets to begin a war, to resist vigorously and successfully any efforts of the U.S.S.R. to expand into areas vital to American security.

The language of military power is the only language which disciples of power politics understand. The United States must use that language in order that Soviet leaders will realize that our government is determined to uphold the interests of its citizens and the rights of small nations. Compromise and concessions are considered, by the Soviets, to be evidences of weakness and they are encouraged by our "retreats" to make new and greater demands.

Demonstrating Military Power

The main deterrent to Soviet attack on the United States, or to attack on areas of the world which are vital to our security, will be the military power of this country. It must be made apparent to the Soviet Government that our strength will be sufficient to repel any attack and sufficient to defeat the U.S.S.R. decisively if a war should start. The prospect of defeat is the only sure means of deterring the Soviet Union.

The Soviet Union's vulnerability is limited due to the vast area over which its key industries and natural resources are widely dispersed, but it is vulnerable to atomic weapons, biological warfare, and long-range air power. Therefore, in order to maintain our strength at a level which will be effective in restraining the Soviet Union, the United States must be prepared to wage atomic and biological warfare. A highly mechanized army, which can be moved either by sea or by air, capable of seizing and holding strategic areas, must be supported by powerful naval and air forces. A war with the U.S.S.R. would be "total" in a more horrible sense than any previous war and there must be constant research for both offensive and defensive weapons.

Whether it would actually be in this country's interest to employ atomic and biological weapons against the Soviet Union in the event of hostilities is a question which would require careful consideration in the light of the circumstances prevailing at the time. The decision would probably be influenced by a number of factors, such as the Soviet Union's capacity to employ similar weapons, which can not now be estimated. But the important point is that the United States must be prepared to wage atomic and biological warfare if necessary. The mere fact of preparedness may be the only powerful deterrent to Soviet aggressive action and in this sense the only sure guaranty of peace.

Protecting U.S. Armaments

The United States, with a military potential composed primarily of highly effective technical weapons, should entertain no proposal for disarmament or limitation of armament as long as the possibility of Soviet aggression exists. Any discussion on the limitation of armaments should be pursued slowly and carefully with the knowledge constantly in mind that proposals on outlawing atomic warfare and long-range offensive weapons would greatly limit United States strength, while only moderately affecting the Soviet Union. The Soviet Union relies primarily on a large infantry and artillery force and the result of such arms limitation would be to deprive the United States of its most effective

Soviet Expansion in Europe 1939–1948

Legend:
- Soviet Union, 1939
- Soviet gains, 1939–1947
- States under Soviet control
- Independent Communist State

weapons without impairing the Soviet Union's ability to wage a quick war of aggression in Western Europe, the Middle East or the Far East.

The Soviet Government's rigid controls on travellers, and its internal security measures, enable it to develop military weapons and build up military forces without our knowledge. The United States should not agree to arms limitations until adequate intelligence of events in the U.S.S.R. is available and, as long as this situation prevails, no effort should be spared to make our forces adequate and strong. Unification of the services and the adoption of universal military training would be strong aids in carrying out a forthright United States policy. In addition to increasing the efficiency of our armed forces, this program would have a salutary psychological effect upon Soviet ambitions.

Comparable to our caution in agreeing to arms limitation, the United States should avoid premature disclosure of scientific and technological information relating to war materiel until we are assured of either a change in Soviet policies or workable international controls. Any disclosure would decrease the advantage the United States now has in technological fields and diminish our strength in relation to that of the U.S.S.R.

Supporting Democratic Nations

In addition to maintaining our own strength, the United States should support and assist all democratic countries which are in any way menaced or endangered by the U.S.S.R. Providing military support in case of attack is a last resort; a more effective barrier to communism is strong economic support. Trade agreements, loans and technical missions strengthen our ties with friendly nations and are effective demonstrations that capitalism is at least the equal of communism. The United States can do much to ensure that economic opportunities, personal freedom and social equality are made possible in countries outside the Soviet sphere by generous financial assistance. Our policy on reparations should be directed toward strengthening the areas we are endeavoring to keep outside the Soviet sphere. Our efforts to break down trade barriers, open up rivers and international waterways, and bring about economic unification of countries, now divided by occupation armies, are also directed toward the reestablishment of vigorous and healthy noncommunist economies.

The Soviet Union recognizes the effectiveness of American economic assistance to small nations and denounces it bitterly by constant propaganda. The United States should realize that Soviet propaganda is dangerous (especially when American "imperialism" is emphasized) and should avoid any actions which give an appearance of truth to the Soviet charges. A determined effort should be made to expose the fallacies of such propaganda.

There are some trouble-spots which will require diligent and considered effort on the part of the United States if Soviet penetration and eventual domination is to be prevented. In the Far East, for example, this country should continue to strive for a unified and economically stable China, a reconstructed and democratic Japan, and a unified and independent Korea. We must ensure Philippine prosperity and we should assist in the peaceful solution, along noncommunistic lines, of the political problems of Southeast Asia and India.

With respect to the United Nations, we are faced with the fact that the U.S.S.R. uses the United Nations as a means of achieving its own ends. We should support the United Nations and all other organizations contributing to international understanding, but if the Soviet Union should threaten to resign at any time because it fails to have its own way, the United States should not oppose Soviet departure. It would be better to continue the United Nations as an association of democratic states than to sacrifice our principles to Soviet threats. . . .

A Coordinated Effort

In conclusion, as long as the Soviet Government adheres to its present policy, the United States should maintain military forces powerful enough to restrain the Soviet Union and to confine Soviet influence to its present area. All nations not now within the Soviet sphere should be given generous economic assistance and political support in their opposition to Soviet penetration. Economic aid may also be given to the Soviet Government and private trade with the U.S.S.R. permitted provided the results are beneficial to our interests and do not simply strengthen the Soviet program. We should continue to work for cultural and intellectual understanding between the United States and the Soviet Union but that does not mean that, under the guise of an exchange program, communist subversion and infiltration in the United States will be tolerated. In order to carry out an effective policy toward the Soviet Union, the United States Government should coordinate its own activities, inform and instruct the American people about the Soviet Union, and enlist their support based upon knowledge and confidence. These actions by the United States are necessary before we shall ever be able to achieve understanding and accord with the Soviet Government on any terms other than its own.

Even though Soviet leaders profess to believe that the conflict between Capitalism and Communism is irreconcilable and must eventually be resolved by the triumph of the latter, it is our hope that they will change their minds and work out with us a fair and equitable settlement when they realize that we are too strong to be beaten and too determined to be frightened.

Viewpoint 3

"United States policy toward the Soviet Union must be that of a long-term, patient but firm and vigilant containment of Russian expansive tendencies."

The United States Should Contain Soviet Expansion

George F. Kennan

George F. Kennan was in charge of long-range planning for the State Department following World War II. In July 1947, having recently returned from the Soviet Union where he had worked at the U.S. embassy in Moscow, Kennan published a letter, "The Sources of Soviet Conduct," under the pseudonym Mr. X in the quarterly journal *Foreign Affairs.*

In the following viewpoint, excerpted from that letter, Kennan argues that a fundamental antagonism between communism and capitalism rule out any lasting cooperation with the Soviet Union; the Soviet Union is a rival, not a partner. Kennan thus opposes appeasement of the Soviet Union and endorses a policy of containment of Soviet expansion. He recommends that the United States apply a "counterforce" at every point where the Soviets threaten to disrupt a peaceful and stable world. Harry S. Truman and Cold War presidents who followed

George F. Kennan, "The Source of Soviet Conduct," *Foreign Affairs*, July 1947.

him adopted Kennan's policy of containment. Kennan remains a respected authority on foreign policy.

The political personality of Soviet power as we know it today is the product of ideology and circumstances: ideology inherited by the present Soviet leaders from the movement in which they had their political origin, and circumstances of power which they now have exercised for nearly three decades in Russia. . . .

Of the original ideology, nothing has been officially junked. Belief is maintained in the basic badness of capitalism, in the inevitability of its destruction, in the obligation of the proletariat to assist in that destruction and to take power into its own hands. But stress has come to be laid primarily on those concepts which relate most specifically to the Soviet regime itself: to its position as the sole truly Socialist regime in a dark and misguided world, and to the relationships of power within it.

The Characteristics of Soviet Policy

The first of these concepts is that of the innate antagonism between capitalism and socialism. We have seen how deeply that concept has become imbedded in foundations of Soviet power. It has profound implications for Russia's conduct as a member of international society. It means that there can never be on Moscow's side any sincere assumption of a community of aims between the Soviet Union and powers which are regarded as capitalist. It must invariably be assumed in Moscow that the aims of the capitalist world are antagonistic to the Soviet regime, and therefore to the interest of the peoples it controls. If the Soviet government occasionally sets its signature to documents which would indicate the contrary, this is to be regarded as a tactical maneuver permissible in dealing with the enemy (who is without honor) and should be taken in the spirit of caveat emptor. Basically, the antagonism remains. It is postulated. And from it flow many of the phenomena which we find disturbing in the Kremlin's conduct of foreign policy: the secretiveness, the lack of frankness, the duplicity, the wary suspiciousness, and the basic unfriendliness of purpose. These phenomena are there to stay, for the foreseeable future. . . .

This means that we are going to continue for a long time to find the Russians difficult to deal with. It does not mean that they should be considered as embarked upon a do-or-die program to overthrow our society by a given date. The theory of the inevitability of the eventual fall of capitalism has the fortunate connotation that there is no hurry about it. The forces of progress can take their time in preparing the final coup de grace. Meanwhile, what is vital is that the "socialist fatherland"—that oasis of power which has been already won for Socialism in their person of the Soviet Union—should be cherished and defended by all good communists at home and abroad, its fortunes promoted, its enemies badgered and confounded. The promotion of premature, "adventuristic" revolutionary projects abroad which might embarrass Soviet power in any way would be an inexcusable, even a counterrevolutionary act. The cause of socialism is the support and promotion of Soviet power, as defined in Moscow.

Infallible Leadership and Iron Discipline

This brings us to the second of the concepts important to contemporary Soviet outlook. That is the infallibility of the Kremlin. The Soviet concept of power, which permits no focal points of organization outside the party itself, requires that the party leadership remain in theory the sole repository of truth. For if truth were to be found elsewhere, there would be justification for its expression in organized activity. But it is precisely that which the Kremlin cannot and will not permit.

The leadership of the Communist Party is therefore always right, and has been always right ever since in 1929 Stalin formalized his personal power by announcing that decisions of the Politburo were being taken unanimously.

On the principle of infallibility there rests the iron discipline of the Communist Party. In fact, the two concepts are mutually self-supporting. Perfect discipline requires recognition of infallibility. Infallibility requires the observance of discipline. And the two together go far to determine the behaviorism of the entire Soviet apparatus of power. But their effect cannot be understood unless a third factor be taken into account: namely, the fact that the leadership is at liberty to put forward for tactical purposes any particular thesis which it finds useful to the cause at any particular moment and to require the faithful and unquestioning acceptance of that thesis by the members of the movement as a whole. This means that truth is not a constant but is actually created, for all intents and purposes, by the Soviet leaders themselves. It may vary from week to week, from month to month. It is nothing absolute and immutable—nothing which flows from objective reality. It is only the most recent manifestation of the wisdom of those in whom the ultimate wisdom is supposed to reside, because they represent the logic of history. The accumulative effect of these factors is to give to the whole subordinate apparatus of Soviet power an unshakable stubbornness and steadfastness in its orientation. . . .

Soviet Patience and Persistence

Thus the Kremlin has no compunction about retreating in the face of superior force. And being under the compulsion of no timetable, it does not get panicky under the necessity for such retreat. Its political action is a fluid stream which moves constantly, wherever it is permitted to move, toward a given goal. Its main concern is to make sure that it has filled every nook and cranny available to it in the basin of world power. But if it finds unassailable barriers in its path, it accepts these philosophically and accommodates itself to them. The main thing is that there should always be pressure, unceasing constant pressure, toward the desired goal. There is no trace of any feeling in Soviet psychology that that goal must be reached at any given time.

These considerations make Soviet diplomacy at once easier and more difficult to deal with than the diplomacy of individual aggressive leaders like Napoleon and Hitler. On the one hand it is more sensitive to contrary force, more ready to yield on individual sectors of the diplomatic front when that force is felt to be too strong, and thus more rational in the logic of rhetoric of power. On the other hand it cannot be easily defeated or discouraged by a single victory on the part of its opponents. And the patient persistence by which it is animated means that it can be effectively countered not by sporadic acts which represent the momentary whims of democratic opinion but only by intelligent long-range policies on the part of Russia's adversaries—policies no less steady in their purpose, and no less variegated and resourceful in their application, than those of the Soviet Union itself.

In these circumstances it is clear that the main element of any United States policy toward the Soviet Union must be that of a long-term, patient but firm and vigilant containment of Russian expansive tendencies. It is important to note, however, that such a policy has nothing to do with outward histrionics: with threats or blustering or superfluous gestures of outward "toughness." While the Kremlin is basically flexible in its reaction to political realities, it is by no means unamenable to considerations of prestige. Like almost any other government, it can be placed by tactless and threatening gestures in a position where it cannot afford to yield even though this might be dictated by its sense of realism. The Russian leaders are keen judges of human psychology, and as such they are highly conscious that loss of temper and of self-control is never a source of strength in political affairs. They are quick to exploit such evidences of weakness. For these reasons, it is a sine qua non of successful dealing with Russia that the foreign government in question should remain at all times cool and collected and that its demands on Russian policy should be put forward in such a manner as to leave the way open for a compliance not too detrimental to Russian prestige.

In the light of the above, it will be clearly seen that the Soviet pressure against the free institutions of the Western world is something that can be contained by the adroit and vigilant application of counter-force at a series of constantly shifting geographical and political points, corresponding to the shifts and maneuvers of Soviet policy, but which cannot be charmed or talked out of existence. The Russians look forward to a duel of infinite duration, and they see that already they have scored great successes. It must be borne in mind that there was a time when the Communist Party represented far more of a minority in the sphere of Russian national life than Soviet power today represents in the world community. . . .

A Rival, Not a Partner

It is clear that the United States cannot expect in the foreseeable future to enjoy political intimacy with the Soviet regime. It must continue to regard the Soviet Union as a rival, not a partner, in the political arena. It must continue to expect that Soviet policies will reflect no abstract love of peace and stability, no real faith in the possibility of a permanent happy coexistence of the Socialist and capitalist worlds, but rather a cautious, persistent pressure toward the disruption and weakening of all rival influence and rival power.

Balanced against this are the facts that Russia, as opposed to the Western world in general, is still by far the weaker party, that Soviet policy is highly flexible, and that Soviet society may well contain deficiencies which will eventually weaken its own total potential. This would of itself warrant the United States entering with reasonable confidence upon a policy of firm containment, designed to confront the Russians with unalterable counter-force at every point where they show signs of encroaching upon the interests of a peaceful and stable world.

Making an Impression

But in actuality the possibilities for American policy are by no means limited to holding the line and hoping for the best. It is entirely possible for the United States to influence by its actions the internal developments, both within Russia and throughout the international communist movement, by which Russian policy is largely determined. This is not only a question of the modest measure of informational activity which this government can conduct in the Soviet Union and elsewhere, although that, too, is important. It is rather a question of the degree to which the United States can create among the peoples of the world generally the impression of a country which knows what it wants, which is coping successfully with the problems of its internal life and with the responsibilities of a world power, and which has a spiritual vitality capable of holding its own among the major ideological currents of the time. To the extent that such an impression can be created and maintained, the aims of Russian communism must appear sterile and quixotic, the hopes and enthusiasm of Moscow's supporters must wane and added strain must be imposed on the Kremlin's foreign policies. For the palsied decrepitude of the capitalist world is the keystone of communist philosophy. Even the failure of the United States to experience the early economic depression which the ravens of the Red Square have been predicting with such complacent confidence since hostilities ceased would have deep and important repercussions throughout the communist world.

By the same token, exhibitions of indecision, disunity and internal disintegration within this country have an exhilarating effect on the whole communist movement. At each evidence of these tendencies, a thrill of hope and excitement goes through the communist world. . . .

Thus the decision will really fall in large measure in this country itself. The issue of Soviet-American relations is in essence a test of the overall worth of the United States as a nation among nations. To avoid destruction the United States need only measure up to its own best traditions and prove itself worthy of preservation as a great nation.

Surely, there was never a fairer test of national quality than this. In the light of these circumstances, the thoughtful observer of Russian-American relations will find no cause for complaint in the Kremlin's challenge to American society. He will rather experience a certain gratitude to a Providence which, by providing the American people with this implacable challenge, has made their entire security as a nation dependent on their pulling themselves together and accepting the responsibilities of moral and political leadership that history plainly intended them to bear.

Viewpoint 4

"The cardinal purpose of the imperialist camp [to which the United States belongs] is to . . . hatch a new imperialist war . . . and to support reactionary and anti-democratic pro-fascist regimes."

The Soviet Union Should Contain U.S. Imperialism

Andrei Zhdanov

Andrei Zhdanov was a Soviet Politburo member and Communist Party leader who Western historians claim was instrumental in formulating an aggressive, anti-Western Soviet foreign policy. In 1947 he organized the Cominform (Communist Information Bureau), which coordinated efforts to spread communism in Europe. In the following viewpoint, excerpted from a report delivered on September 22, 1947, at Cominform's first conference, Zhdanov stresses the ideological differences between the United States and the Soviet Union and the need to resist imperialist expansion.

According to Zhdanov, the Soviet Union is a peace-seeking nation that hopes to share its progressive, superior social system—communism—with the world. Unlike the Soviet Union, which respects the sovereignty of nations, imperialist nations such as the United States impose their capitalistic ideologies on

Andrei Zhdanov, "Report on the International Situation to the Cominform," September 22, 1947.

46

oppressed countries worldwide, he maintains. In fact, he asserts, imperialist nations are anti-democratic whereas the Soviet Union stands for democracy. Nevertheless, claims Zhdanov, the Soviet Union does not seek war with the United States; it seeks to coexist in peace.

The fundamental changes caused by the war [World War II] on the international scene and in the position of individual countries has entirely changed the political landscape of the world. A new alignment of political forces has arisen. The more the war recedes into the past, the more distinct becomes two major trends in postwar international policy, corresponding to the division of the political forces operating on the international arena into two major camps: the imperialist and anti-democratic camp, on the one hand, and the anti-imperialist and democratic camp, on the other. The principal driving force of the imperialist camp is the U.S.A. Allied with it are Great Britain and France. . . . The imperialist camp is also supported by colony-owning countries, such as Belgium and Holland, by countries with reactionary anti-democratic regimes, such as Turkey and Greece, and by countries politically and economically dependent upon the United States, such as the Near Eastern and South American countries and China.

Two Major Postwar Camps

The cardinal purpose of the imperialist camp is to strengthen imperialism, to hatch a new imperialist war, to combat socialism and democracy, and to support reactionary and anti-democratic pro-fascist regimes and movements everywhere.

In the pursuit of these ends the imperialist camp is prepared to rely on reactionary and anti-democratic forces in all countries, and to support its former adversaries in the war against its wartime allies.

The anti-fascist forces comprise the second camp. This camp is based on the U.S.S.R. and the new democracies. It also includes countries that have broken with imperialism and have firmly set foot on the path of democratic development, such as Rumania, Hungary and Finland. Indonesia and Vietnam are associated with it; it has the sympathy of India, Egypt and Syria. The anti-imperialist camp is backed by the labor and democratic movement and by the fraternal Communist parties in all countries, by the fighters for national liberation in the colonies and dependencies, by all progressive and democratic forces in every country. The purpose of this camp is to resist the threat of new wars and imperialist expansion, to strengthen democracy and to extirpate the vestiges of fascism.

The Goals of the Soviet State

The end of the Second World War confronted all the freedom-loving nations with the cardinal task of securing a lasting demo-

Stalin Responds to Churchill's "Iron Curtain" Speech

In the following excerpt from his interview with the Russian newspaper Pravda, *Soviet leader Joseph Stalin responds to former British prime minister Winston Churchill's famous "iron curtain" speech delivered at Westminster College in Fulton, Missouri, on March 5, 1946. In the speech, Churchill argued that Europe was divided by an iron curtain separating free democratic nations from totalitarian Communist countries. He urged the United States and Great Britain to unite in protecting democratic nations from Communist tyranny.*

Hitler began to set war loose by announcing his racial theory, declaring that only people speaking the German language represent a fully valuable nation. Mr. Churchill begins to set war loose, also by a racial theory, maintaining that only nations speaking the English language are fully valuable nations, called upon to decide the destinies of the entire world.

The German racial theory brought Hitler and his friends to the conclusion that the Germans, as the only fully valuable nation, must rule over other nations. The English racial theory

cratic peace sealing victory over fascism. In the accomplishment of this fundamental task of the postwar period the Soviet Union and its foreign policy are playing a leading role. This follows from the very nature of the Soviet socialist state, to which motives of aggression and exploitation are utterly alien, and which is interested in creating the most favorable conditions for the building of a communist society. One of these conditions is external peace. As embodiment of a new and superior social system, the Soviet Union reflects in its foreign policy the aspirations of progressive mankind, which desires lasting peace and has nothing to gain from a new war hatched by capitalism. The Soviet Union is a staunch champion of liberty and independence of all nations, and

---

brings Mr. Churchill and his friends to the conclusion that nations speaking the English language, being the only fully valuable nations, should rule over the remaining nations of the world. . . .

As a result of the German invasion, the Soviet Union has irrevocably lost in battles with the Germans, and also during the German occupation and through the expulsion of Soviet citizens to German slave labor camps, about 7,000,000 people. In other words, the Soviet Union has lost in men several times more than Britain and the United States together.

It may be that some quarters are trying to push into oblivion these sacrifices of the Soviet people which insured the liberation of Europe from the Hitlerite yoke.

But the Soviet Union cannot forget them. One can ask therefore, what can be surprising in the fact that the Soviet Union, in a desire to ensure its security for the future, tries to achieve that these countries should have governments whose relations to the Soviet Union are loyal? How can one, without having lost one's reason, qualify these peaceful aspirations of the Soviet Union as "expansionist tendencies" of our Government?

Joseph Stalin, *Pravda*, March 14, 1946.

a foe of national and racial oppression and colonial exploitation in any shape or form. The change in the general alignment of forces between the capitalist world and the socialist world brought about by the war has still further enhanced the significance of the foreign policy of the Soviet state and enlarged the scope of its activity on the international arena.

The successes and the growing international prestige of the democratic camp were not to the liking of the imperialists. Even while World War II was still on, reactionary forces in Great Britain and the United States became increasingly active, striving to prevent concerted action by the Allied powers, to protract the war, to bleed the U.S.S.R., and to save the fascist aggressors from utter defeat. The sabotage of the Second Front, [the Soviet Union's military drive against Nazi Germany from the east] by the Anglo-Saxon imperialists, headed by [British prime minister Winston] Churchill, was a clear reflection of this tendency, which was in point of fact a continuation of the Munich policy[1] in the new and changed conditions. But while the war was still in progress British and American reactionary circles did not venture to come out openly against the Soviet Union and the democratic countries, realizing that they had the undivided sympathy of the masses all over the world. But in the concluding months of the war the situation began to change. The British and American imperialists already manifested their willingness to respect the legitimate interests of the Soviet Union and the democratic countries at the Potsdam tripartite [Britain, the Soviet Union, and the United States] conference in July 1945.

A Quest for Peace

The foreign policy of the Soviet Union and the democratic countries in these two past years has been a policy of consistently working for the observance of the democratic principles in the postwar settlement. The countries of the anti-imperialist camp have loyally and consistently striven for the implementation of these principles,

1. A 1938 treaty signed in Munich by Britain, France, Germany, and Italy. The pact represented the high point of the policy of appeasement of Nazi Germany and Fascist Italy by Britain and France before World War II. Its immediate result was the dismemberment of Czechoslovakia.

without deviating from them one iota. Consequently, the major objective of the postwar foreign policy of the democratic states has been a democratic peace, the eradication of the vestiges of fascism and the prevention of a resurgence of fascist imperialist aggression, the recognition of the principle of the equality of nations and respect for their sovereignty, and general reduction of all armaments and the outlawing of the most destructive weapons, those designed for the mass slaughter of the civilian population. . . .

Of immense importance are the joint efforts of the diplomacy of the U.S.S.R. and that of the other democratic countries to secure a reduction of armaments and the outlawing of the most destructive of them—the atomic bomb.

Soviet foreign policy proceeds from the fact of the coexistence for a long period of the two systems—capitalism and socialism. From this it follows that cooperation between the U.S.S.R. and countries with other systems is possible, provided that the principle of reciprocity is observed and that obligations once assumed are honored. Everyone knows that the U.S.S.R. has always honored the obligations it has assumed. The Soviet Union has demonstrated its will and desire for cooperation.

Viewpoint 5

"There was a system-wide Soviet bloc threat with a significant amount of unity."

Soviet Expansion Policies Initiated the Cold War

Douglas J. Macdonald

Cold War scholars who study the war's origins fall into three general categories: traditionalists, who believe that Soviet expansion precipitated the Cold War; revisionists, who claim that U.S. hostility toward communism led to the Cold War; and post-revisionists, who argue that mutual misperceptions led to shared responsibility for the Cold War. Over the years, many Cold War scholars have dismissed the traditionalist argument. However, in the following viewpoint, Douglas J. Macdonald, professor of political science at Colgate University in Hamilton, New York, argues that post–Cold War evidence supports the traditional view that the Soviet Union's foreign policy led to Cold War hostilities. Macdonald cites evidence that the Soviet Union dictated policy in Communist-bloc nations across Europe and Asia to refute claims that fears about Soviet expansion were unwarranted. The Soviet Union, he concludes, was indeed a threat, and U.S. policy makers were prudent in developing strategies to contain Communist expansion.

Douglas J. Macdonald, "Communist Bloc Expansion in the Early Cold War: Challenging Realism, Refuting Revisionism," *International Security*, vol. 20, Winter 1995. Copyright © 2003 by the President and Fellows of Harvard College. Reproduced by permission of The MIT Press, Cambridge, MA.

Was there ever a unified communist threat facing the United States during the Cold War? Or did U.S. decision-makers misperceive Soviet and communist bloc "defensiveness" and "caution" as expansionist threats? Did U.S. leaders, realizing that the Soviets and their ideological allies posed no security threat to the United States and its allies, create such claims for various domestic political reasons? Such questions have dominated analyses of the Cold War in the United States [since the 1960s]. To the surprise of some and the consternation of others, the demise of the Cold War and the resulting flow of new evidence from the East in recent years has reinvigorated many of these arguments over its origins, the primary responsibility for its creation, and U.S. actions during that era. The Cold War is over, but the controversies surrounding it and its meaning for contemporary scholarship and policy are not. . . .

The Historical Debate

As with many historical events, a Hegelian[1] pattern of argumentation—thesis or traditional view, antithesis or revisionist view, and synthesis or post-revisionist view—developed for analyses of the Cold War. The traditional view of the Cold War held that the Soviet Union was an expansionist nation primarily responsible for political and military contention, and that there was a real and global communist threat to independent but internally weak nations, both those that ringed the Soviet Union in Europe, the Middle East, and Asia in the aftermath of World War II and the emerging new nations. U.S. security policies were therefore mostly reasonable and necessary, or at the least understandable and defensible. The Soviet Union, according to this view, headed a grouping of ideologically like-minded revolutionary entities and nations that were actively expansionist through the selective support of non-ruling communist parties in their quests for power. The essence of the early Cold War was that the Soviet Union and its ideological clients were united and expansionist, and that the

1. Georg Wilhelm Friedrich Hegel (1770–1831) was a prominent German philosopher who developed the theory of historical analysis illustrated here. Those who followed Hegel's ethical and social philosophy, including Karl Marx, often became revolutionaries.

United States was relatively slow in reacting to the global nature of the threat posed by that expansion. It was only checked when the West, and especially the United States, took strong, unified stands against the Soviet Union to contain it.

Beginning in the mid-1960s, largely in reaction to the Vietnam War, a revisionist school evolved among U.S. historians who proposed that the United States was primarily to blame for the Cold War. U.S. leaders were driven by an unreasonable hostility to communism, largely generated by domestic political and economic needs. Since the Soviets had at most only tenuous influence over communist groups, U.S. actions during the Cold War, especially in the Third World, were unnecessary and overdone, even at times criminal. In this view, the United States was seen as actively expansionist, while the Soviet Union was simply responding to U.S. provocations. These starkly drawn arguments affected much of U.S. historiography of the Cold War until the 1980s. In general, traditional analysis defended U.S. and Western containment policies; revisionism rejected them.

In the later years of the Cold War, there were attempts to forge a post-revisionist synthesis by historians, the foremost among them John Lewis Gaddis. The post-revisionists essentially accepted U.S. European policy while separating it sharply from U.S. Third World policies. This allowed them to avoid having to defend the Vietnam War and other policies of which they disapproved. They accepted some U.S. responsibility for the Cold War and were strongly critical of U.S. interventions in the developing nations, for example, yet found credible the Soviet threat to Europe and Japan. The post-revisionists tried to strike a balance between traditionalism and revisionism and to stake out a middle ground based on mutual misperception, mutual reactivity, and shared responsibility between the superpowers. Borrowing insights from the psychological decision-making and realist literatures in political science, there was sometimes a strong emphasis on a supposedly consistent misperception of political and power realities by all concerned.

Alternative Theories

Some historians who reject the traditional stance from an allegedly realist or post-revisionist perspective, such as historian Melvyn

Leffler in his award-winning history of the origins of the Cold War, *A Preponderance of Power*, have also fixed primary blame for the globalization of the Cold War on U.S. anticommunism and the resulting flawed processes of determining threats. The Cold War, according to Leffler, was largely caused by the actions of the United States, with the Soviets largely responding defensively to U.S. initiatives: "Soviet actions were reactive." Although Leffler at times ascribes mutuality of responsibility to the superpowers, Anders Stephanson correctly notes that in this widely acclaimed work, "the case is closed: the United States initiated the Cold War, the Soviet Union did not."

Post-revisionism was supported in important ways by the criticisms of U.S. policies emanating from the dominant paradigm of the political science subdiscipline of international relations, realism, which posits the non-ideological pursuit of power as the basis for international relations. According to realists, it is the competition over capabilities among states that determines policies. This view suggests that the spread of communism presented little threat to the United States because nationalism and self-interest, not communist ideology, are what drive states to act. Nationalism prevented a coordination of international policies by these governments. The actions of each are therefore only properly understood sui generis. There was no Soviet bloc unified by ideology in the early Cold War period, according to this view; there were only discrete states seeking individual versions of their national interests defined in terms of power. Such a state of anarchy in international politics produces the security dilemma: each state is ultimately left to its own resources to protect itself, but as each tries to do so it alarms other states that are also seeking to protect themselves. Realist analysts portray a world of endemic misperceptions within the context of the constant struggle over power. This view complements the post-revisionist view of mutual reactivity between the superpowers and joint responsibility in the early Cold War.

The Emergence of New Evidence

In this debate, the traditionalist position has been under-represented in recent decades and dealt with as a straw man. Historiographic discussions rarely mention traditionalist works written after 1970, and those prior to that year are often portrayed as "of mostly archaeological interest now," [writes Anders Stephanson]. This has recently begun to change. Largely drawing on the unprecedented level of materials being declassified and released from communist archives, as well as increasingly candid interviews with policymakers of the former Soviet Union and the People's Republic of China, new interpretations are emerging that can be characterized as traditionalist in orientation, in their views on the new empirical findings if not yet in analytical and historiographical coherence. Divergent interpretations of the Cold War are again in lively contention.

The primary reason for this resurgence of the traditional viewpoint is that a good deal of the new evidence has not been kind to post-revisionist, realist, and especially revisionist analyses. It turns out that even ardent U.S. Cold-Warriors such as [former U.S. secretary of state] John Foster Dulles were far more sophisticated in their view of the communist threat than their public rhetoric would suggest; that ideology was an important factor in decision-making for the Soviet Union and its potential allies, especially in the early Cold War, and that the communist world coordinated expansionist policies far more than believed by many critics of U.S. policies. This is creating a new look at how U.S. decision-makers perceived threats during the Cold War. Some post-revisionist analysts have partly incorporated these insights into their work. John Lewis Gaddis, for example, has recently declared that "American policy-makers at no point during the postwar era actually believed in the existence of an international communist monolith." Some new interpretations suggest that U.S. and Western decision-makers were not that far off in their perceptions of the threat posed by the Soviet bloc, at least in the early period. Even the common view that NSC 68 [a National Security Council report to President Harry S. Truman] was an irrational call to arms based on pure ideology, or a cynical ploy to scare people, is being questioned by some scholars, and that document is being portrayed as a more rational depiction of actual threats facing the West than previously believed.

In sum, traditionalists portray the Soviet Union as an expansionist, ideologically driven power and the West as primarily reactive; revisionists argue that the Soviets were reactive, and the United States expansionist; post-revisionists, while assigning some responsibility for the Cold War to Soviet expansionist pressures, often place equal or greater blame on the United States; realists portray the Soviets as highly reactive because of the security dilemma, and therefore generally defensive and cautious. Determining whether the Soviet Union was an actively expansionist power is thus essential to ascertaining responsibility for the origins of the Cold War, the plausibility of Western threat perceptions, the accuracy of realist theories, and the defensibility of the resulting containment policies.

A Widespread Fear of Soviet Expansion

Although many critics of the Cold War concentrate their attention on alleged U.S. misperceptions of Soviet expansion, it is worth noting that most other non-communist nations shared these perceptions in the early Cold War with unusual consensus. This included not only governments but also many groups not afraid to criticize the United States or to attempt to get along with the Soviets, such as the British Labour Party or the French Socialists. Even such an unexpected source as [British writer and philosopher] Bertrand Russell wondered aloud whether a preemptive attack on Stalin might not be necessary in the 1940s. This particularly challenges those analysts who utilize cognitive theories of decision-making and domestic politics explanations for U.S. foreign policy. Many such critics emphasize Soviet defensiveness, caution, and decidedly limited aims, disparaging the very notion of a unified communist bloc. . . .

Given the fact that most other non-communists widely viewed Soviet actions in the early Cold War as threatening to Western interests, analyses that focus solely on the psychology of U.S. decision-makers and their domestic political machinations cannot explain the causes of this phenomenon. By concentrating on internal causation, recent critiques of U.S. policies give the erroneous impression that the fear of communist bloc expansion was largely, if not exclusively, in the minds of U.S. decision-makers.

While an analysis that includes allied perceptions challenges the other explanations of the Cold War, it is necessary but insufficient

to confirm a traditional interpretation. That these threat perceptions were widely shared does not necessarily prove that the threat
was therefore objectively defined. But such analysis does properly
shift the focus of attention to where the best evidence is to be
found for testing the "unified Soviet bloc" thesis of traditionalism. What needs to be assessed further is whether these shared
threat perceptions had a basis in reality, or were erroneous or
greatly exaggerated as the critics charge.

Soviet Control of Bloc Policy

The U.S. standard for judging coordination of Soviet bloc policies
assumed a considerable degree of Soviet control of the direction
of international policies in intra-bloc and extra-bloc relations. This
control over bloc policies, however, should not be viewed as day-
to-day, monolithic control of all actions taken by bloc members:
despite some of their public rhetoric, U.S. leaders did not view the
situation in this way. Revisionists, post-revisionists, and realists all
argue, although for different reasons, that the assumption of Soviet leadership of a communist bloc was greatly exaggerated by
traditionalist scholars. Indeed, if there is a single issue that most
distinguishes these schools from the traditional view, it is the
posited existence of a relatively unified bloc acting in concert. Thus
the critics predict only low levels of effort by the Soviets to aid individual communist groups and a high degree of independence of
action by all communists at the international and local levels,
while traditionalists predict relatively generous support and a high
degree of coordination of policies under Soviet strategic direction.
What must be examined is the degree of control over the general
direction of bloc policies, that is, the ability of the Soviet Union to
shape the behavior of lesser members, especially revolutionary or
foreign policies. There are few real puppets in international politics, but there are leaders and followers. . . .

Both ruling and non-ruling parties closely coordinated their
policies with Soviet international lines in the early Cold War and
did so to a degree that warranted the suspicion that the Soviets
had control over those policies. The case of Titoism is instructive
in this regard, and was used by Western decision-makers as an important measure of fealty to Moscow's direction of bloc policy.

[Communist Yugoslavia's leader] Marshal Tito was charged by the Soviets with the crime of nationalism because he would not allow Stalinist agents (a major means of ensuring that ideologically friendly factions rose to the top) to roam freely in Yugoslavia. All ruling and non-ruling parties stepped into line in condemning what should have been seen as relatively minor challenges to Soviet leadership if the assumption of independence were applicable. For example, the Chinese, despite their reputation for subsequent independence from Moscow, went out of their way to reassure Stalin of their loyalty to Soviet-led internationalism. Though some critics have pointed to Tito as an example of the lack of Soviet control over bloc policies, he was the exact opposite: the exception that supports the rule. Within that context, Soviet dictates along international lines had to be followed or a party ran the risk of being labelled "Titoist." Criticism of Titoism, then, was a crude but accurate indicator of adherence to Stalin's international policy directions.

More reasonable standards must be found to describe these power relationships and measure the degree of international coordination of communist policies during the Cold War. On balance, the circumstantial evidence suggests that Western officials' perceptions of the Soviet bloc and traditional analyses of the Soviet threat were more correct than those of many subsequent critics. A relatively high degree of Soviet control over bloc members' policies, especially relations with other bloc nations and other international policies, but also often a Stalinist-inspired orthodoxy internally, was a consistent reality for most members in the early years of the Cold War. . . .

Spreading the Revolution

Many revisionist, post-revisionist, and realist critics of U.S. policies have questioned whether there was a direct Soviet role in initiating the invasion of South Korea by Kim Il Sung's regime in 1950 and in China's adoption of a role as Soviet surrogate among Asian communist parties. Traditionalists have argued that the Soviets played a direct role in the Korean War, and that they designated the Chinese as the bloc's representative in supporting revolution in Southeast Asia. The new evidence on the Soviet role in

Korea and the Chinese role in Vietnam strongly supports a traditionalist interpretation of bloc expansion.

Revisionist historians such as Robert Simmons and Bruce Cumings have argued for a high degree of independence of action for the northern regime, and Samuel Wells has made the realist argument that the decision for war was primarily Chinese and Korean, thereby challenging the traditional view of Soviet bloc leadership. These views are no longer credible. As Sergei Goncharov, John Lewis, and Xue Litai conclude in their path-breaking work based on a great deal of new evidence, the North Korean invasion was "preplanned, blessed, and directly assisted by Stalin and his generals, and reluctantly backed by Mao at Stalin's insistence."

Stalin personally informed Kim Il Sung, formerly both a member of the CCP [Chinese Communist Party] and an officer in the Soviet army, and Ho Chi Minh, a former member of the CCP and a Comintern agent for nearly thirty years, of the change to a militant policy and the new Chinese role as bloc leader in the region in early 1950. The Chinese combat role in Korea is well known. It has also long been known that the Soviets and Chinese supplied the North Koreans in their attempt to take over the South. The question that deserves new attention is the role of the Soviets in initiating and participating in the hostilities.

North Korea Was a Soviet Satellite

The new evidence demonstrates conclusively that North Korea was a satellite of the Soviet Union. Soviet control over Kim's revolutionary policy was such that it could prevent him from attacking the South or allow him to do so at will: the North Koreans had wanted to attack as early as the spring of 1949 but had to wait until the Soviets gave their permission and material support in the spring of 1950. Once the decision was made, the Chinese and Soviet supply effort to the North Koreans was massive. The detailed plans for the invasion were drawn up by the Soviets and then communicated to the Koreans. The North Koreans never took any major actions without first consulting with the Soviets. The Soviets were not only not surprised by the timing of the attack, as often claimed, but helped choose its date and timing. Soviet advisers in Korea played crucial roles in executing the invasion in its early stages. By any reasonable measurement, this is an unusually high degree of control over the freedom of action of another state. Most of the major claims of the revisionists, post-revisionists, and realists on Soviet-Korean relations are thus largely incorrect, and most of those of the traditionalists essentially sound.

Moreover, the Soviet actions in support of the Koreans included a direct role in the fighting that was far greater than previously known in the West: a total of 70,000 Soviet pilots, gunners, and technicians served in Korea, and claimed to have shot down a total of 569 allied aircraft. Elaborate precautions were typically taken to cover the Soviet military role, such as Soviet soldiers dressing in Chinese uniforms and attempting to speak only in the Korean language during air operations. The Soviets played a similar clandestine role in the Vietnam War in the mid-1960s. It can no longer be stated categorically that the superpowers never directly fought one another in the Cold War. Yet some revisionist authors play down the Soviet actions in Korea in the face of extensive evidence to the contrary, calling them defensive, "modest," insignificant, or not indicative of Soviet expansionist designs because they were "unofficial."

In their new role as bloc leader in the region, the Chinese began a large-scale effort in Indochina to support the Viet Minh under the leadership of Ho Chi Minh, as well as to help the Vietnamese reorganize the Cambodian and Laotian communists who had been members of the Indochinese Communist Party in the 1930s. This was done for a mixture of security and ideological purposes. Cold War critics portrayed these actions as minimal and ineffective, but the new evidence emerging from China challenges this notion. Direct Chinese aid to the Vietnamese was critical to their military victory over the French, as was Soviet aid to the Chinese in their civil war, just as traditionalist scholarship suggested. . . .

The Soviet Union Was a Threat

U.S. and other Western leaders did not misperceive either the actions or the intentions of the Soviet Union and other communists in the early Cold War. Much of the newly available evidence confirms many traditionalist analytical assumptions about bloc expansion, in particular that there was a system-wide Soviet bloc threat with a significant amount of unity, and that this bloc was both held together and driven to expand its sphere of influence by the shared totalist ideological tenets of Marxism-Leninism, largely as defined in Moscow. . . .

The revisionist paradigm for understanding the Cold War has failed the test of the new evidence. In particular, the view of the Soviet Union and other communist nations as inherently cautious status-quo powers is not tenable. Stalin's vaunted caution was caused by the very Western containment policies in Europe and the Middle East that the revisionists blame for the Cold War. In Asia, the one region where there was no early unified Western response, the Soviets and their ruling and non-ruling bloc clients planned and attempted revolutionary uprisings on a region-wide scale in an ideologically driven power move. Revisionists cannot explain this coordinated expansionism. They instead portray any such moves as strictly based in local conditions with little Soviet or Chinese direction or even input. Soviet control over ruling bloc members' international policies and non-ruling bloc members' revolutionary policies in the Stalinist period was at times monolithic, at times not, but it was almost always great. Western threat perceptions of a militant, revolutionary grouping under Stalin's international leadership were therefore justified. The new evidence demonstrates conclusively that the revisionists have been wide of the mark in their efforts to explain the Soviet Union, other Marxist-Leninists, and the Cold War.

Viewpoint 6

"Primary responsibility for the cold war . . . lies with the United States because it was the first state to shift to hard-line policies."

U.S. Containment Policies Initiated the Cold War

Dale C. Copeland

Scholars who study the origins of the Cold War fall into three camps: traditionalists argue that Soviet expansion precipitated the Cold War; revisionists claim that U.S. hostility toward communism led to the Cold War; and post-revisionists maintain that mutual misperceptions led to shared responsibility for the Cold War. Although Dale C. Copeland, professor of foreign affairs at the University of Virginia, agrees with the post-revisionist view that both the United States and the Soviet Union share responsibility for the Cold War, in the following viewpoint he argues that the United States was the first to adopt hard-line policies against its adversary and is therefore largely responsible for initiating the war. In Copeland's view the Soviet Union shifted to a policy of confrontation only when provoked by President Harry S. Truman's containment strategy, which included surrounding the Soviet Union with U.S. air and naval bases, using the atomic bomb, refusing to share atomic secrets, and denying the Soviets a role in the occupation of Japan, Russia's longtime enemy. Truman's decisions during the summer of 1945 could only have been seen by the Soviet Union as a threat to its security.

Three main perspectives have dominated the debate on the origins of the cold war. For traditionalists the cold war was caused by hostile Soviet intentions rooted in communist ideology and the need to justify internal repression. Once Soviet expansionist goals became clear in 1946 and 1947, the United States was forced into a firm containment posture that it would otherwise have avoided. The revisionists turn this argument on its head, arguing that the origins of the cold war lie in hostile U.S. actions from 1945 to 1947, at a point when Soviet leaders sought peace so that they could rebuild their devastated country. The reasons revisionists give for U.S. aggression vary, but they include American efforts to promote global capitalism and American paranoia in regard to U.S. security needs. The third perspective, postrevisionism, offers a middle-ground position. Postrevisionists hold that the cold war was, above all, the tragic result of the anarchic international system. Both superpowers were driven primarily by the quest for security; yet, each saw the other as aggressive, and thus each acted to protect its respective sphere. These actions fueled an unnecessary spiral of mistrust and hostility, one that persisted into the 1980s.

Hard-Line Policies

This essay, building on the seminal work of Melvyn Leffler in 1992, agrees with the postrevisionist argument but pushes it a bit further. By 1946–1947 both superpowers were indeed caught up in a tragic spiral of distrust. Primary responsibility for the cold war, however, lies with the United States because it was the first state to shift to hard-line policies after the Second World War. As early as mid 1945 President Harry S Truman began to move toward a policy that later became known as "containment," despite his awareness that this policy would likely lead to a destabilizing arms race. He took this provocative action, Leffler argues, to ensure that the United States maintained its "preponderance of power" against the rising Soviet colossus. Containment strategies in 1945 thus reflected rational geopolitics rather than greed or irrational paranoia.

Truman's adoption of hard-line policies was not based on a belief that Soviet premier Joseph Stalin had aggressive intentions. In fact, Truman liked and even respected Stalin at that time. Rather, Truman recognized that if America did not act, the Soviet Union would grow significantly, and the Soviet leaders who later replaced Stalin might not be so moderate. In short, the cold war began for

The Complexity of Cold War Origins

In the following excerpt John Lewis Gaddis, a prolific Cold War author and well-regarded proponent of the post-revisionist school of thought concerning the origins of the Cold War, summarizes his views on the complexities that led to the Cold War.

The Cold War grew out of a complicated interaction of external and internal developments inside both the United States and the Soviet Union. The external situation—circumstances beyond the control of either power—left Americans and Russians facing one another across prostrated Europe at the end of World War II. Internal influences in the Soviet Union—the search for security, the role of ideology, massive postwar reconstruction needs, the personality of Stalin—together with those in the United States—the ideal of self-determination, fear of communism, the illusion of omnipotence fostered by American economic strength and the atomic bomb—made the resulting confrontation a hostile one. Leaders of both superpowers sought peace, but in doing so yielded to considerations which, while they did not precipitate war, made a resolution of differences impossible.

John Lewis Gaddis, *The United States and the Origins of the Cold War, 1941–1947*. New York: Columbia University Press, 1972.

systemic, realistic reasons: the fear of decline; uncertainty about the future intentions of the other nation; and the prudent realization that unless preventive action were taken at that time, it might be too late in the future.

Restricting Soviet Growth

Standard accounts of the cold war usually designate 1947 as the year in which the American containment strategy was set in place. Yet, the core foundations of this containment were actually laid by August 1945. The full extent of this policy may be seen in the following eight interlocking actions taken in 1945 to restrict Soviet economic and military growth:

1. The surrounding of the Soviet Union with U.S. air and naval bases in order to project military power into the Soviet heartland;
2. the termination of U.S. aid to the Soviets, even as aid was extended to the Chinese—an action that included resisting Soviet claims to badly needed reparations from Germany;
3. the use of the atomic bomb, which—in addition to ending the Pacific war quickly—was designed to make Moscow more accommodating in postwar relations;
4. the American effort to rebuild western Europe, which required the revitalization of the western half of Germany, a nation that had just killed more than twenty million Russians;
5. the rapid deployment of U.S. and allied troops in Korea, China, and Manchuria to prevent communist penetration of the region;
6. the U.S. refusal to give atomic secrets and materials to the Soviet Union;
7. the restricting of Soviet naval access to the Mediterranean and North Sea despite recognition of Soviet legal rights;
8. the exclusion of any Soviet role in the occupation and revitalization of Japan, a nation that had fought several wars with Russia in the first half of the twentieth century.

A Necessary Risk?

In implementing this policy Truman did not believe he was abandoning all chances of cooperation with the Soviet Union; a great-power modus vivendi might still be worked out. Any such arrangement, however, would be on U.S. terms. In short, the United States would do everything necessary to maintain a preponderant position. If the Soviets cooperated, so much the better. If they did not, Truman preferred a cold war—with all its attendant risks of inadvertent escalation—to a situation in which the United States cooperated at the expense of long-term power. Allowing the Soviet Union to achieve a dominant position would threaten U.S. security, should Soviet intentions prove aggressive down the road.

On 2 April 1945 a top-secret report from the Office of Strategic Services (OSS), forerunner of the Central Intelligence Agency (CIA), was forwarded to President [Franklin D.] Roosevelt; it was subsequently given to Truman. The report outlined the dilemma: Russia would emerge from the war as the strongest nation in Eurasia. Indeed, "Russia's natural resources and manpower are so great that within a relatively few years she can be much more powerful than either Germany or Japan has ever been. In the easily foreseeable future Russia may well outrank even the United States in military potential." These fears were reinforced by similar OSS intelligence reports in May. Later that month James F. Byrnes, who was soon to be secretary of state, summed up the feelings of Truman's inner circle. He argued that the best U.S. strategy would be to push ahead as quickly as possible in the development of atomic weaponry to ensure that America stayed ahead of the Soviet Union, even as the United States tried to maintain good relations.

An Uncertain Future

The tragic side of U.S. policy in 1945 is that it sprang from a fear of future Soviet intentions, not present ones. During the Potsdam Conference[1] in July–August 1945, as he crystallized his containment strategy, Truman found Stalin not entirely disagreeable. In late July he wrote in his diaries and to his wife that he liked Stalin and found him honest and straightforward. Near the end of the conference Stalin canceled a meeting because of a cold, and Truman wrote in

---

1. At the Potsdam Conference, Britain, the Soviet Union, and the United States divided post–World War II Germany into four occupation zones, administered by Britain, France, the United States, and the Soviet Union.

a diary entry that he was worried about what would happen were Stalin suddenly to die. Some "demagogue on horseback" would take over the Soviet state and destroy the fragile European peace. Byrnes expressed similar concerns throughout the fall of 1945.

Maintaining the U.S. preponderance of power was thus considered necessary as protection against an uncertain future. Yet, U.S. leaders also understood that the policies required to secure this preponderance could antagonize Moscow. In discussions over the spring and summer with his old friend Joseph E. Davies, a former ambassador to the Soviet Union, Truman was warned repeatedly that, given their history, the Russians were extremely anxious about foreign attacks. In particular Davies cautioned that the demonstration of atomic weaponry over Japan and the withholding of atomic secrets would only undermine Soviet trust, causing a massive arms race that might lead to nuclear annihilation. Yet, by the fall of 1945 Truman's sense of prudence had led him to reject all atomic sharing. In October an old friend, Fyke Farmer, asked him if this policy meant that the armaments race was on. The president replied in the affirmative, but added that the United States would stay ahead.

It is now generally accepted that at least part of the reason for dropping atomic bombs on Japan was to send a signal of U.S. superiority to Moscow. In particular Byrnes and Secretary of War Henry L. Stimson believed in the summer of 1945 that demonstrating the effectiveness of the bomb would impress Russia with American military might. Byrnes thought the atomic bomb might help to keep the Soviets from overwhelming Manchuria and northern China in August. After the mid-July atomic tests revealed the true destructive power of the bomb, Truman was much more confident that it could be employed as a diplomatic tool to restrict Soviet expansion. As he told an assistant at Potsdam, the bomb "would keep the Russians straight." This conviction made him more willing to press U.S. demands at the conference, which could only have heightened growing Soviet suspicions.

A Reaction to Containment Policy?

Nothing in the foregoing argument implies that the Soviet Union was a "good" state; it was, as Truman realized, a brutal dictatorship that killed and oppressed its own citizens. Yet, out of simple geopolitical self-interest, Stalin wanted to maintain good relations with the West in 1945: he needed breathing space to rebuild his war-ravaged country. Loans from the United States, reparations from Germany, and relative peace in the near term were critical to this rebuilding process. It is thus not surprising that Truman found Stalin straightforward and businesslike at Potsdam. Yet, it is evident that after August, once the elements of Truman's containment policy were in place, Moscow became much less accommodating. Stalin pressed for early development of a Soviet atomic bomb, sought to prevent Soviet exclusion from the occupation of Japan, and resisted any Soviet retreat from northern Iran. By 1946 Soviet rhetoric was predicting that a clash between the two superpowers was all but inevitable.

In the end, of course, it is difficult to say whether, even without the provocative U.S. actions in 1945, the Soviets would have shifted to a policy of confrontation. Stalin and his advisers were a highly suspicious, if not paranoid, lot. It is clear, however, that in terms of relative hostility of policy, the United States moved first in the escalation spiral. Although the Soviets did seek to consolidate their hold in eastern Europe, both Roosevelt and Truman in 1945 had resigned themselves to the division of Europe. Yet, the series of actions Truman undertook during the summer of 1945 could only have been seen by Moscow as an effort to project superior American power against the Soviet periphery and to maintain U.S. strategic preponderance.

American policy was not immoral, only tragic. It reflected the twin problems of the fear of decline and the fear of future intentions of the rising Soviet state. In such circumstances it was only prudent for the stronger state to move reluctantly to shore up its dominance across the board. Truman's understanding that his policies would likely bring on a cold-war spiral only heightens the sense of tragedy. He was forced to choose a policy that represented the lesser of two evils: preponderance and an increased risk of war in the short term over decline and a possible war later under less auspicious power conditions.

CHAPTER 2

Coexistence and Conflict

✳ Chapter Preface

It was once said that the sun never set on the British Empire. World War II, however, weakened the colonial powers—particularly Britain and France. The colonies themselves, aware of this growing weakness, began advocating independence, and liberation movements within these developing nations began to evolve. U.S. foreign policy makers encouraged U.S. intervention in these movements to prevent Communist revolutions, thereby hoping to prevent the spread of Soviet influence. Whether this intervention was justified or effective was hotly debated throughout the Cold War and after.

In February 1956 Soviet premier Nikita Khrushchev delivered a secret speech at the twentieth Congress of the Communist Party of the Soviet Union in which he promised that the Soviet Union would support "wars of national liberation." The Soviet Union had good reasons to assist developing nations struggling to be free of their colonial powers. Such assistance would enable the Soviets to expand their sphere of influence and strengthen communism worldwide without risking a direct attack on the democratic West, which would likely result in nuclear retaliation.

Another reason that the Soviets chose to actively encourage developing nations to reject capitalism in favor of communism was to facilitate the demise of capitalism, which had not failed as quickly as many Communists had anticipated. Karl Marx, the German socialist philosopher who inspired Soviet communism, had prophesied that the exploited masses in capitalist countries would soon reach a breaking point and reject the free market system. Despite these predictions, capitalism thrived. Fortunately for the Soviets, developing nations, long oppressed by capitalist colonial powers, could often be persuaded to accept the Communist model.

Taking these factors into account, many commentators conclude that U.S. leaders had good reason to believe that the Soviet Union was in a good position to extend its sphere of influence in developing regions throughout the world, such as Asia, Africa, and Latin America. In consequence, according to historians Dennis E.

71

Showalter and Paul DuQuenoy, "The U.S. government . . . began a massive campaign to prevent countries in the Third World from adopting a communist system and supporting the policies of the Soviet Union. This campaign took many forms: economic aid; political support of authoritarian, anticommunist rulers; covert action; and military intervention." Supporters of U.S. intervention contend that these efforts helped keep Soviet power in check and enhance America's security.

However, some commentators believe these efforts were costly and unnecessary. They refute the reasons cited to support U.S. intervention in the internal affairs of developing nations. For example, historian Benjamin Frankel contests the claim that developing nations were economically important to the United States. He maintains that most of these nations were of no economic value: "Most were so poor that they were a net drain rather than a net gain to whichever superpower won their allegiance." Moreover, Frankel argues, it was not in the interest of these struggling nations to deny the West access to their resources. In fact, he writes, "the history of communist and communist-leaning regimes . . . shows that they actively sought economic relations with Western countries."

Frankel also disputes the claim that a failure to intervene would create the impression that the United States would not defend its strategically important interests and that Americans lacked the resolve to battle communism. Frankel argues that in fact America's willingness to counter every move the Soviets made in developing countries actually made it more difficult to take action in these regions when absolutely necessary, making the United States appear weak. Involvement in Vietnam, for example, resulted in what he calls the Vietnam Syndrome: "Tired of the bloodshed and waste in the Vietnam War (ended 1975) and disenchanted with foreign involvement, American public opinion made it difficult for decision makers to send U.S. troops overseas even when there was a good cause to do so."

Lastly, Frankel disputes the claim that U.S. intervention helped spread democratic values and principles. In its fight against communism, Frankel asserts, the United States often supported repressive non-Communist regimes that opposed reform. Frankel cites, for example, Rafael Trujillo Molina of the Dominican Republic, the Samoza family in Nicaragua, and military juntas in Chile, Brazil, Argentina, Uruguay, and El Salvador as convincing examples of tyrannical regimes that garnered U.S. support. He writes, "At least in Latin America, most U.S. interventionism was done in support of repressive regimes, not of democratic values."

Whether or not U.S. intervention in the liberation movements of developing nations was worth the cost remains the subject of debate. In the following chapter, authors examine U.S. and Soviet foreign policy decisions made during the 1950s and 1960s—a period of coexistence and conflict.

Viewpoint 1

"As military action is confined to [Korea's] territorial limits, it condemns that nation, which it is our purpose to save."

The War in Korea Should Be Expanded

Douglas MacArthur

Douglas MacArthur, a popular World War II military leader, was named commander of the UN military forces sent to defend South Korea after the June 25, 1950, invasion by Communist North Korea. When MacArthur drove Chinese-assisted North Korean forces to the Chinese border, China intervened and drove UN forces back to the original border of North and South Korea. MacArthur believed that UN forces should bomb Chinese military installations and enlist the aid of U.S.-supported Nationalist Chinese forces in Formosa (Taiwan), led by Chiang Kai-shek, who had been ousted from mainland China in 1949 by the Communist Chinese. President Harry Truman disagreed with this strategy; he hoped to limit the war to Korea and avoid direct conflict with China or the Soviet Union. Nevertheless, MacArthur continued—publicly—to defend his position, and Truman relieved MacArthur of his command on April 11, 1951. In the following viewpoint, taken from an address before a joint session of Congress on April 19, 1951, MacArthur defends his position that to ensure success in the Cold War, U.S. military

Douglas MacArthur, address to a joint session of Congress, Washington, DC, April 19, 1951.

policy in Korea and all of Asia should aim toward total victory against Communist aggression.

I do not stand here as advocate for any partisan cause, for the issues are fundamental and reach quite beyond the realm of partisan consideration. They must be resolved on the highest plane of national interest if our course is to prove sound and our future protected. I trust, therefore, that you will do me the justice of receiving that which I have to say as solely expressing the considered viewpoint of a fellow American. I address you with neither rancor nor bitterness in the fading twilight of life with but one purpose in mind, to serve my country.

The issues are global and so interlocked that to consider the problems of one sector oblivious to those of another is but to court disaster for the whole.

A Global Threat

While Asia is commonly referred to as the gateway to Europe, it is no less true that Europe is the gateway to Asia, and the broad influence of the one cannot fail to have its impact upon the other.

There are those who claim our strength is inadequate to protect on both fronts, that we cannot divide our effort. I can think of no greater expression of defeatism. If a potential enemy can divide his strength on two fronts, it is for us to counter his effort.

The Communist threat is a global one. Its successful advance in one sector threatens the destruction of every other sector. You cannot appease or otherwise surrender to communism in Asia without simultaneously undermining our efforts to halt its advance in Europe.

Beyond pointing out these general truisms, I shall confine my discussion to the general areas of Asia. Before one may objectively assess the situation now existing there, he must comprehend something of Asia's past and the revolutionary changes which have marked her course up to the present. Long exploited by the so-called colonial powers, with little opportunity to achieve any degree of social justice, individual dignity, or a higher standard of life such as guided our own noble administration of the Philippines, the peoples of Asia found their opportunity in the war just past to throw off the shackles of colonialism and now see the dawn of new opportunity and heretofore unfelt dignity and the self-respect of political freedom.

A New Force

Mustering half of the earth's population and 60 percent of its natural resources these peoples are rapidly consolidating a new force, both moral and material, with which to raise the living standard and erect adaptations of the design of modern progress to their own distinct cultural environments. Whether one adheres to the concept of colonialization or not, this is the direction of Asian progress and it may not be stopped. It is a corollary to the shift of the world economic frontiers, as the whole epi-center of world affairs rotates back toward the area whence it started. In this situation it becomes vital that our own country orient its policies in consonance with this basic evolutionary condition rather than pursue a course blind to the reality that the colonial era is now past and the Asian peoples covet the right to shape their own free destiny. What they seek now is friendly guidance, understanding, and support, not imperious direction; the dignity of equality, not the shame of subjugation. Their prewar standard of life, pitifully low, is infinitely lower now in the devastation left in war's wake. World ideologies play little part in Asian thinking and are little understood. What the peoples strive for is the opportunity for a little more food in their stomachs, a little better clothing on their backs, a little firmer roof over their heads, and the realization of a normal nationalist urge for political freedom. These political-social conditions have but an indirect bearing upon our own national security, but do form a backdrop to contemporary planning which must be thoughtfully considered if we are to avoid the pitfalls of unrealism.

Defending the Pacific

Of more direct and immediate bearing upon our national security are the changes wrought in the strategic potential of the Pacific Ocean in the course of the past war. Prior thereto, the western strategic frontier of the United States lay on the littoral line of the Americas with an exposed island salient extending out through Hawaii, Midway, and Guam to the Philippines. That salient proved not an outpost of strength but an avenue of weakness along which the enemy could and did attack. The Pacific was a potential area of advance for any predatory force intent upon striking at the bordering land areas.

All this was changed by our Pacific victory. Our strategic frontier then shifted to embrace the entire Pacific Ocean which became a vast moat to protect us as long as we held it. Indeed, it acts as a protective shield for all of the Americas and all free lands of the Pacific Ocean area. We control it to the shores of Asia by a chain of islands extending in an arc from the Aleutians to the Marianas held by us and our free allies.

From this island chain we can dominate with sea and air power every Asiatic port from Vladivostok to Singapore and prevent any hostile movement into the Pacific. Any predatory attack from Asia must be an amphibious effort. No amphibious force can be successful without control of the sea lanes and the air over those lanes in its avenue of advance. With naval and air supremacy and modest ground elements to defend bases, any major attack from continental Asia toward us or our friends of the Pacific would be doomed to failure. Under such conditions the Pacific no longer represents menacing avenues of approach for a prospective invader—it assumes instead the friendly aspect of a peaceful lake. Our line of defense is a natural one and can be maintained with a minimum of military effort and expense. It envisions no attack against anyone nor does it provide the bastions essential for offensive operations, but properly maintained would be invincible defense against aggression.

Preventing a Breach

The holding of this littoral defense line in the western Pacific is entirely dependent upon holding all segments thereof, for any major breach of that line by an unfriendly power would render vulnerable to determined attack every other major segment. This is a military estimate as to which I have yet to find a military leader who will take exception.

For that reason I have strongly recommended in the past as a matter of military urgency that under no circumstances must Formosa fall under Communist control.

Such an eventuality would at once threaten the freedom of the

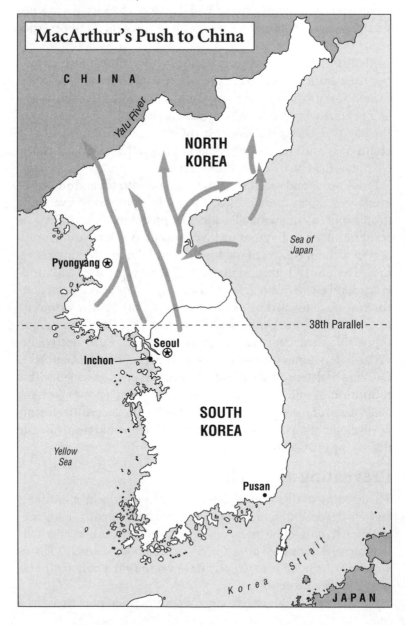

Philippines and the loss of Japan, and might well force our western frontier back to the coasts of California, Oregon, and Washington. . . .

On Formosa, the Government of the Republic of China has had the opportunity to refute by action much of the malicious gossip which so undermined the strength of its leadership on the Chinese mainland.

The Formosan people are receiving a just and enlightened administration with majority representation in the organs of government; and politically, economically, and socially appear to be advancing along sound and constructive lines.

The Korean Conflict

With this brief insight into the surrounding areas I now turn to the Korean conflict. While I was not consulted prior to the President's decision to intervene in the support of the Republic of Korea, that decision from a military standpoint proved a sound one. As I say, a brief and sound one as we hurled back the invaders and decimated his forces. Our victory was complete and our objectives within reach when Red China intervened with numerically superior ground forces. This created a new war and an entirely new situation, a situation not contemplated when our forces were committed against the North Korean invaders, a situation which called for new decisions in the diplomatic sphere to permit the realistic adjustment of military strategy. Such decisions have not been forthcoming.

While no man in his right mind would advocate sending our ground forces into continental China—and such was never given a thought—the new situation did urgently demand a drastic revision of strategic planning if our political aim was to defeat this new enemy as we had defeated the old.

Apart from the military need as I saw it to neutralize sanctuary, protection given to the enemy north of the Yalu, I felt that military necessity in the conduct of the war made necessary:

First, the intensification of our economic blockade against China.

Second, the imposition of a naval blockade against the China coast.

Third, removal of restrictions on air reconnaissance of China's coastal areas and of Manchuria.

Fourth, removal of restrictions on the forces of the Republic of China on Formosa with logistical support to contribute to their effective operation against the Chinese mainland.

The Price of Command

For entertaining these views, all professionally designed to support our forces committed to Korea and bring hostilities to an end with the least possible delay and at a saving of countless American and Allied lives, I have been severely criticized in lay circles, principally abroad, despite my understanding that from a military standpoint the above views have been fully shared in the past by practically every military leader concerned with the Korean campaign, including our own Joint Chiefs of Staff.

I called for reinforcements, but was informed that reinforcements were not available. I made clear that if not permitted to utilize the friendly Chinese force of some 600,000 men on Formosa; if not permitted to blockade the China coast to prevent the Chinese Reds from getting succor from without; and if there were to be no hope of major reinforcements, the position of the command from the military standpoint forbade victory. We could hold in Korea by constant maneuver and at an approximate area where our supply advantages were in balance with the supply line disadvantages of the enemy, but we could hope at best for only an indecisive campaign, with its terrible and constant attrition upon our forces if the enemy utilized his full military potential. I have constantly called for the new political decisions essential to a solution. Efforts have been made to distort my position. It has been said in effect that I was a warmonger. Nothing could be further from the truth. I know war as few other men now living know it, and nothing to me is more revolting. . . .

The Importance of Victory

But once war is forced upon us, there is no other alternative than to apply every available means to bring it to a swift end. War's very object is victory—not prolonged indecision. In war, indeed, there can be no substitute for victory.

There are some who for varying reasons would appease Red China. They are blind to history's clear lesson. For history teaches with unmistakable emphasis that appeasement but begets new and bloodier war. It points to no single instance where the end has justified that means—where appeasement has led to more than a sham peace. Like blackmail, it lays the basis for new and successively greater demands, until, as in blackmail, violence becomes the only other alternative. Why, my soldiers asked of me, surrender military advantages to an enemy in the field? I could not answer. Some may say to avoid spread of the conflict into an all-out war with China; others, to avoid Soviet intervention. Neither explanation seems valid. For China is already engaging with the maximum power it can commit and the Soviet will not necessarily mesh its actions with our moves. Like a cobra, any new enemy will more likely strike whenever it feels that the relativity in military or other potential is in its favor on a world-wide basis.

The tragedy of Korea is further heightened by the fact that as military action is confined to its territorial limits, it condemns that nation, which it is our purpose to save, to suffer the devastating impact of full naval and air bombardment, while the enemy's sanctuaries are fully protected from such attack and devastation. Of the nations of the world, Korea alone, up to now, is the sole one which has risked its all against communism. The magnificence of the courage and fortitude of the Korean people defies description. They have chosen to risk death rather than slavery. Their last words to me were "Don't scuttle the Pacific."

I have just left your fighting sons in Korea. They have met all tests there and I can report to you without reservation they are splendid in every way. It was my constant effort to preserve them and end this savage conflict honorably and with the least loss of time and a minimum sacrifice of life. Its growing bloodshed has caused me the deepest anguish and anxiety. Those gallant men will remain often in my thoughts and in my prayers always.

Viewpoint 2

"The course we have been following [in Korea] is the one best calculated to avoid an all-out war."

The War in Korea Should Be Limited

Harry S. Truman

On June 25, 1950, Communist North Korea invaded democratic South Korea. U.S. president Harry S. Truman convinced the United Nations (UN) to condemn North Korea's attack and send UN forces, composed largely of U.S. troops, to defend South Korea. Under the leadership of World War II hero U.S. general Douglas MacArthur, UN forces drove the North Koreans to the Chinese border. China then entered the war, forcing UN forces back to the original North and South Korean border, where both sides remained in a bloody stalemate.

MacArthur recommended that UN forces bomb military installations in China and engage the help of U.S.-supported Nationalist Chinese forces led by Chiang Kai-shek, who had been ousted from mainland China in 1949 by Chinese Communists. Truman disagreed; he argued that defending South Korea was necessary to deter Communist aggression, but he argued against expanding the war by attacking China. Truman did not want to risk an all-out war with China or the Soviet Union. When MacArthur continued to publicly defend his views, Truman relieved him of command on April 11, 1951. In the following

Harry S. Truman, address to the people of the United States, April 11, 1951.

viewpoint, taken from his address to the American people that day, Truman defends his policy in Korea and his unpopular decision to remove the beloved general.

The Communists in the Kremlin are engaged in a monstrous conspiracy to stamp out freedom all over the world. If they were to succeed, the United States would be numbered among their principal victims. It must be clear to everyone that the United States cannot—and will not—sit idly by and await foreign conquest. The only question is: When is the best time to meet the threat and how?

The best time to meet the threat is in the beginning. It is easier to put out a fire in the beginning when it is small than after it has become a roaring blaze.

And the best way to meet the threat of aggression is for the peace-loving nations to act together. If they don't act together, they are likely to be picked off, one by one. . . .

The Lessons of History

If history has taught us anything, it is that aggression anywhere in the world is a threat to peace everywhere in the world. When that aggression is supported by the cruel and selfish rulers of a powerful nation who are bent on conquest, it becomes a clear and present danger to the security and independence of every free nation.

This is a lesson that most people in this country have learned thoroughly. This is the basic reason why we joined in creating the United Nations. And since the end of World War II we have been putting that lesson into practice—we have been working with other free nations to check the aggressive designs of the Soviet Union before they can result in a third world war. . . .

The aggression against Korea is the boldest and most dangerous move the Communists have yet made.

The attack on Korea was part of a greater plan for conquering all of Asia. . . .

The question we have had to face is whether the Communist plan of conquest can be stopped without general war. Our Government and other countries associated with us in the United Nations believe that the best chance of stopping it without general war is to meet the attack in Korea and defeat it there.

That is what we have been doing. It is a difficult and bitter task. But so far it has been successful.

So far, we have prevented World War III.

So far, by fighting a limited war in Korea, we have prevented aggression from succeeding and bringing on a general war. And the ability of the whole free world to resist Communist aggression has been greatly improved.

We have taught the enemy a lesson. He has found out that aggression is not cheap or easy. Moreover, men all over the world who want to remain free have been given new courage and new hope. They know now that the champions of freedom can stand up and fight and that they will stand up and fight.

Our resolute stand in Korea is helping the forces of freedom now fighting in Indochina and other countries in that part of the world. It has already slowed down the timetable of conquest.

In Korea itself, there are signs that the enemy is building up his ground forces for a new mass offensive. We also know that there have been large increases in the enemy's available air forces.

If a new attack comes, I feel confident it will be turned back. The United Nations fighting forces are tough and able and well equipped. They are fighting for a just cause. They are proving to all the world that the principle of collective security will work. We are proud of all these forces for the magnificent job they have done against heavy odds. We pray that their efforts may succeed, for upon their success may hinge the peace of the world.

The Communist side must now choose its course of action. The Communist rulers may press the attack against us. They may take further action which will spread the conflict. They have that choice, and with it the awful responsibility for what may follow. The Communists also have the choice of a peaceful settlement which could lead to a general relaxation of tensions in the Far East. The decision is theirs, because the forces of the United Nations will strive to limit the conflict if possible.

We do not want to see the conflict in Korea extended. We are trying to prevent a world war—not to start one. The best way to do that is to make it plain that we and the other free countries will continue to resist the attack.

Preventing World War III

But you may ask: Why can't we take other steps to punish the aggressor? Why don't we bomb Manchuria and China itself? Why don't we assist Chinese Nationalist troops to land on the mainland of China?

If we were to do these things we would be running a very grave risk of starting a general war. If that were to happen, we would have brought about the exact situation we are trying to prevent.

If we were to do these things, we would become entangled in a vast conflict on the continent of Asia and our task would become immeasurably more difficult all over the world.

What would suit the ambitions of the Kremlin better than for our military forces to be committed to a full-scale war with Red China?

It may well be that, in spite of our best efforts, the Communists may spread the war. But it would be wrong—tragically wrong—for us to take the initiative in extending the war.

The dangers are great. Make no mistake about it. Behind the North Koreans and Chinese Communists in the front lines stand additional millions of Chinese soldiers. And behind the Chinese stand the tanks, the planes, the submarines, the soldiers, and the scheming rulers of the Soviet Union.

Our aim is to avoid the spread of the conflict.

The Best Course of Action

The course we have been following is the one best calculated to avoid an all-out war. It is the course consistent with our obligation to do all we can to maintain international peace and security. Our experience in Greece and Berlin shows that it is the most effective course of action we can follow.

First of all, it is clear that our efforts in Korea can blunt the will of the Chinese Communists to continue the struggle. The United Nations forces have put up a tremendous fight in Korea and have inflicted very heavy casualties on the enemy. Our forces are stronger now than they have been before. These are plain facts which may discourage the Chinese Communists from continuing their attack.

Second, the free world as a whole is growing in military strength every day. In the United States, in Western Europe, and throughout the world, free men are alert to the Soviet threat and are building their defenses. This may discourage the Communist rulers from continuing the war in Korea—and from undertaking new acts of aggression elsewhere.

If the Communist authorities realize that they cannot defeat us in Korea, if they realize it would be foolhardy to widen the hostilities beyond Korea, then they may recognize the folly of continuing their aggression. A peaceful settlement may then be possible. The door is always open.

Then we may achieve a settlement in Korea which will not compromise the principles and purposes of the United Nations.

I have thought long and hard about this question of extending the war in Asia. I have discussed it many times with the ablest military advisers in the country. I believe with all my heart that the course we are following is the best course.

I believe that we must try to limit the war to Korea for these vital reasons: to make sure that the precious lives of our fighting men are not wasted; to see that the security of our country and the free world is not needlessly jeopardized; and to prevent a third world war.

A Change in Command

A number of events have made it evident that General [Douglas] MacArthur did not agree with that policy. I have therefore considered it essential to relieve General MacArthur so that there would be no doubt or confusion as to the real purpose and aim of our policy.

It was with the deepest personal regret that I found myself compelled to take this action. General MacArthur is one of our greatest military commanders. But the cause of world peace is more important than an individual.

The change in commands in the Far East means no change whatever in the policy of the United States. We will carry on the fight in Korea with vigor and determination in an effort to bring the war to a speedy and successful conclusion. . . .

In the meantime, I want to be clear about our military objective. We are fighting to resist an outrageous aggression in Korea. We are trying to keep the Korean conflict from spreading to other areas. But at the same time we must conduct our military activities so as to insure the security of our forces. This is essential if they are to continue the fight until the enemy abandons its ruthless attempt to destroy the Republic of Korea.

That is our military objective—to repel attack and to restore peace.

In the hard fighting in Korea, we are proving that collective action among nations is not only a high principle but a workable means of resisting aggression. Defeat of aggression in Korea may be the turning point in the world's search for a practical way of achieving peace and security.

The struggle of the United Nations in Korea is a struggle for peace.

The free nations have united their strength in an effort to prevent a third world war.

That war can come if the Communist rulers want it to come. But this Nation and its allies will not be responsible for its coming.

We do not want to widen the conflict. We will use every effort to prevent that disaster. And in so doing we know that we are following the great principles of peace, freedom, and justice.

Viewpoint 3

"Peaceful coexistence can and should develop into peaceful competition for the purpose of satisfying man's needs in the best possible way."

The Soviet Union Seeks Peaceful Coexistence with the United States

Nikita Khrushchev

After Joseph Stalin's death on March 5, 1953, Nikita Khrushchev emerged as Communist Party leader and later premier of the Soviet Union. Khrushchev denounced Stalin and his policies, and he instituted a program of "destalinization" that restored legal procedures, reduced the threat of the secret police, closed labor camps, and to some degree restored public debate.

Soviet relations with the rest of the world also changed under the leadership of Khrushchev. Although Khrushchev believed that communism would ultimately triumph over capitalism, he advocated peaceful coexistence with the West, a policy he explains in the following viewpoint. According to Khrushchev, the principle of peaceful coexistence contains two pledges: to resolve differences without war and to renounce interference with the

Nikita Khrushchev, "On Peaceful Coexistence," *Foreign Affairs*, vol. 38, October 1959. Copyright © 1959 by the Council of Foreign Relations, Inc. Reproduced by permission.

internal affairs of other countries. The Soviet Union, Khrushchev claims, seeks victory over capitalism not through acts of aggression but through cooperative competition, which will allow the people of the world to see the advantages of communism.

I have been told that the question of peaceful coexistence of states with different social systems is uppermost today in the minds of many Americans—and not only Americans. The question of coexistence, particularly in our day, interests literally every man and woman on the globe.

We all of us well know that tremendous changes have taken place in the world. Gone, indeed, are the days when it took weeks to cross the ocean from one continent to the other or when a trip from Europe to America, or from Asia to Africa, seemed a very complicated undertaking. The progress of modern technology has reduced our planet to a rather small place; it has even become, in this sense, quite congested. And if in our daily life it is a matter of considerable importance to establish normal relations with our neighbors in a densely inhabited settlement, this is so much the more necessary in the relations between states, in particular, states belonging to different social systems.

You may like your neighbor or dislike him. You are not obliged to be friends with him or visit him. But you live side by side, and what can you do if neither you nor he has any desire to quit the old home and move to another town? All the more so in relations between states. It would be unreasonable to assume that you can make it so hot for your undesirable neighbor that he will decide to move to Mars or Venus. And vice versa, of course.

The Fear of Peaceful Coexistence

What, then, remains to be done? There may be two ways out: either war—and war in the rocket and H-bomb age is fraught with the most dire consequences for all nations—or peaceful coexistence. Whether you like your neighbor or not, nothing can be done about it, you have to find some way of getting on with him, for you both live on one and the same planet.

But the very concept of peaceful coexistence, it is said, by its alleged complexity frightens certain people who have become unaccustomed to trusting their neighbors and who see a double bottom in each suitcase. People of this kind, on hearing the word "coexistence," begin to play around with it in one way and another, sizing it up and applying various yardsticks to it. Isn't it a fraud? Isn't it a trap? Does not coexistence signify the division of the world into areas separated by high fences, which do not communicate with each other? And what is going to happen behind those fences?

The more such questions are piled up artificially by the cold-war mongers, the more difficult it is for the ordinary man to make head or tail of them. It would therefore be timely to rid the essence of this question of all superfluous elements and to attempt to look soberly at the most pressing problem of our day—the problem of peaceful competition.

The Rise of a New Social System

One does not need to delve deeply into history to appreciate how important it is for mankind to ensure peaceful coexistence. And here it maybe said parenthetically that the European might have benefited a great deal in their day if, instead of organizing senseless crusades which invariably ended in failure, they had established peaceful relations with the differently-minded peoples of the Moslem East.

But let us turn to facts concerning the relatively recent past when the watershed between states no longer consisted of different religious creeds and customs, but of much deeper differences of principle relating to the choice of social systems. This new situation arose on the threshold of the 1920s when, to the booming of the guns of the Russian cruiser *Aurora* which had joined the rebellious workers and peasants, a new and unprecedented social system, a state of workers and peasants, came into the world.

Its appearance was met with the disgruntled outcries of those who naïvely believed the capitalist system to be eternal and immutable. Some people even made an attempt to strangle the unwanted infant in the cradle. Everybody knows how this ended: our people voted with their arms for Soviet power, and it came to stay. And even then, in 1920, V.I. Lenin, replying to the question of an

American correspondent as to what basis there could be for peace between Soviet Russia and America, said: "Let the American imperialists not touch us. We won't touch them."

From its very inception the Soviet state proclaimed peaceful coexistence as the basic principle of its foreign policy. It was no accident that the very first state act of the Soviet power was the decree on peace, the decree on the cessation of the bloody war.

Defining Peaceful Coexistence

What, then, is the policy of peaceful coexistence?

In its simplest expression it signifies the repudiation of war as a means of solving controversial issues. However, this does not cover the entire concept of peaceful coexistence. Apart from the commitment to non-aggression, it also presupposes an obligation on the part of all states to desist from violating each other's territorial integrity and sovereignty in any form and under any pretext whatsoever. The principle of peaceful coexistence signifies a renunciation of interference in the internal affairs of other countries with the object of altering their system of government or mode of life or for any other motives. The doctrine of peaceful coexistence also presupposes that political and economic relations between countries are to be based upon complete equality of the parties concerned, and on mutual benefit.

It is often said in the West that peaceful coexisting is nothing else than a tactical method of the socialistic states. There is not a grain of truth in such allegations. Our desire for peace and peaceful coexistence is not conditioned by any time-serving or tactical considerations. It springs from the very nature of socialist society in which there are no classes or social groups interested in profiting by war or seizing and enslaving other people's territories. The Soviet Union and the other socialist countries, thanks to their socialist system, have an unlimited home market and for this reason they have no need to pursue an expansionist policy of conquest and an effort to subordinate other countries to their influence.

It is the people who determine the destinies of the socialist states. The socialist states are ruled by the working people themselves, the workers and peasants, the people who themselves create all the material and spiritual values of society. And people of labor cannot want war. For to them war spells grief and tears, death, devastation and misery. Ordinary people have no need for war.

From Coexistence to Cooperation

Contrary to what certain propagandists hostile to us say, the co-existence of states with different social systems does not mean that they will only fence themselves off from one another by a high wall and undertake the mutual obligation not to throw stones over the wall or pour dirt upon each other. No! Peaceful coexistence does not mean merely living side by side in the absence of war but with the constantly remaining threat of its breaking out in the future. *Peaceful coexistence can and should develop into peaceful competition for the purpose of satisfying man's needs in the best possible way.*

We say to the leaders of the capitalist states: Let us try out in practice whose system is better, let us compete without war. This is much better than competing in who will produce more arms and who will smash whom. We stand and always will stand for such competition as will help to raise the well-being of the people to a higher level.

The principle of peaceful competition does not at all demand that one or another state abandon the system and ideology adopted by it. It goes without saying that the acceptance of this principle cannot lead to the immediate end of disputes and contradictions which are inevitable between countries adhering to different social systems. But the main thing is ensured: the states which decided to adopt the path of peaceful coexistence repudiate the use of force in any form and agree on a peaceful settlement of possible disputes and conflicts, bearing in mind the mutual interests of the parties concerned. In our age of the H-bomb and atomic techniques this is the main thing of interest to every man. . . .

Victory Without War

We Communists believe that the idea of Communism will ultimately be victorious throughout the world, just as it has been victorious in our country, in China and in many other states. Many readers of *Foreign Affairs* will probably disagree with us. Perhaps they think that the idea of capitalism will ultimately triumph. It is their right to think so. We may argue, we may disagree with one another. *The main thing is to keep to the positions of ideological struggle, without resorting to arms in order to prove that one is right.* The point is that with military techniques what they are today, there are no inaccessible places in the world. Should a world war break out, no country will be able to shut itself off from a crushing blow.

We believe that ultimately that system will be victorious on the globe which will offer the nations greater opportunities for improving their material and spiritual life. It is precisely socialism that creates unprecedentedly great prospects for the inexhaustible creative enthusiasm of the masses, for a genuine flourishing of science and culture, for the realization of man's dream of a happy life, a life without destitute and unemployed people, of a happy childhood and tranquil old age, of the realization of the most audacious and ambitious human projects, of man's right to create in a truly free manner in the interests of the people.

But when we say that in the competition between the two systems, the capitalist and the socialist, our system will win, this does not mean, of course, that we shall achieve victory by interfering in the internal affairs of the capitalist countries. Our confidence in the victory of Communism is of a different kind. It is based on a knowledge of the laws governing the development of society. Just as in its time capitalism, as the more progressive system, took the place of feudalism, so will capitalism be inevitably superseded by Communism—the more progressive and more equitable social system. We are confident of the victory of the socialist system because it is a more progressive system than the capitalist system. . . .

A Stable Peace

Peaceful coexistence is the only way which is in keeping with the interests of all nations. To reject it would mean under existing conditions to doom the whole world to a terrible and destructive war at a time when it is fully possible to avoid it.

Is it possible that when mankind has advanced to a plane where it has proved capable of the greatest discoveries and of making its first steps into outer space, it should not be able to use the colossal achievements of its genius for the establishment of a stable peace, for the good of man, rather than for the preparation of another war and for the destruction of all that has been created by its labor over many millenniums? Reason refuses to believe this. It protests.

The Soviet people have stated and declare again that they do not want war. If the Soviet Union and the countries friendly to it are not attacked, we shall never use any weapons either against the United States or against any other countries. We do not want any horrors of war, destruction, suffering and death for ourselves or for any other peoples. We say this not because we fear anyone. Together with our friends, we are united and stronger than ever. But precisely because of that do we say that war can and should be prevented. Precisely because we want to rid mankind of war, we urge the Western powers to peaceful and lofty competition. We say to all: Let us prove to each other the advantages of one's own system not with fists, not by war, but by peaceful economic competition in conditions of peaceful coexistence.

As for the social system in some state or other, that is the domestic affair of the people of each country. We always have stood and we stand today for non-interference in the internal affairs of other countries. We have always abided, and we shall abide, by these positions. The question, for example, of what system will exist in the United States or in other capitalist countries cannot be decided by other peoples or states. This question can and will be decided only by the American people themselves, only by the people of each country.

The existence of the Soviet Union and of the other socialist countries is a real fact. It is also a real fact that the United States of America and the other capitalist countries live in different social conditions, in the conditions of capitalism. Then let us recognize this real situation and proceed from it in order not to go against reality, against life itself. Let us not try to change this situation by interferences from without, by means of war on the part of some states against other states.

I repeat, there is only one way to peace, one way out of the existing tension: peaceful coexistence.

Viewpoint 4

"It is clear that when Communists employ the language of 'peace,' they do so to mask their true strategic purpose: the isolation, encirclement, weakening, and final destruction of the free world."

The Soviet Union Does Not Seek Peaceful Coexistence with the United States

Richard V. Allen

Nikita Khrushchev reformed many of Joseph Stalin's rigid and oppressive domestic and foreign policies when he became Soviet premier in 1958. Khrushchev advocated a policy of "peaceful coexistence" with the West. American opinion differed on whether the policy of "peaceful coexistence" was a step toward ending the Cold War or whether it was simply a strategy designed to keep the United States off guard.

In the following viewpoint, excerpted from his 1964 book, *Peaceful Coexistence: A Communist Blueprint for Victory*, foreign policy analyst Richard V. Allen cautions against misreading the intentions of the Communists. Allen concludes that the Soviet Union's real motive is not to seek genuine peace but to weaken and destroy the free world. Allen later served as a presidential assistant to Richard Nixon and as national security adviser to President Ronald Reagan in 1981–1982.

T raditionally, Communists have always given the greatest care to defining carefully the strategic course of action to be followed over a given period of time. Tactics may vary within the period of time in which the strategy operates, but the latter will remain constant until officially changed and until that change has been proclaimed to the world movement. . . .

A Strategy to Overthrow the Free World

Is "peaceful coexistence" a strategy or a tactic?

> The Marxist-Leninists do not understand the policy of peaceful coexistence as a tactical maneuver designed for some limited span of time, but as the strategic line designed for the whole period of the transition from capitalism to socialism on a world scale. (*Pravda*, December 6, 1963)

Peaceful coexistence is therefore the strategy which will carry forth the Communist revolution to the final overthrow of the free world and the establishment of worldwide Communist rule. To take it as something less important than the "strategic line," or to dismiss it as a "semantic phrase" would be to ignore the fundamental statement of the plan to accomplish the final phase of the attack against the non-Communist world.

As the principal "strategic line" of the majority of the Communist movement, peaceful coexistence is quite young. It received its initial, cautious formulation and blessing by [Soviet premier Nikita] Khrushchev at the Twentieth Party Congress in 1956, but escaped widespread attention in the West because of the sensational nature of the "de-Stalinization" pronouncements made at that time. It was [Soviet premier Joseph] Stalin, however, who first affirmed that "coexistence" was a temporary possibility designed to buy time. Speaking at the Fifteenth Congress of the Communist Party of the Soviet Union in 1927, he said that

The period of "peaceful coexistence" is receding into the past, giving way to a period of imperialist attacks. . . . Hence our task is to pay attention to contradictions in the capitalist camp, to delay war by "buying off" the capitalists and to take all measures to maintain peaceful relations. . . . Our relations with the capitalist countries are based on the assumption that the coexistence of the two opposing systems is possible. Practice has fully confirmed this.

Still earlier references to coexistence may be found in [the head of Russian revolutionary leaders Leon] Trotsky and [Vladimir] Lenin, but until recent years it has been a descriptive slogan; i.e., it described a condition to which, however unfortunate for the Communists, they had to adapt.

Under conditions of obvious inferiority to the "capitalist world," until 1956 the Communists described their position as one of "capitalist encirclement." The major task under those conditions, according to Stalin, was to strike incessantly at the "weakest link" of the capitalist chain in an effort to break out of the "encirclement." At the Twentieth Party Congress the declaration was made that the chain had been broken, and that the worldwide revolution had begun to enter the final phase of human history, the "transition from capitalism to socialism on a worldwide scale." It is in this phase that the Communists relinquish the defensive position assumed under the previous conditions of peaceful coexistence, and go over to the strategic offensive under a new and enriched kind of peaceful coexistence.

While the phraseology has undergone no change—i.e., "peaceful coexistence" is still used to describe Communist policy objectives—the content of the slogan has changed radically to accommodate the new period of the offensive. Thus it is that the period of peaceful coexistence contains such nonpeaceful events as the construction of the Berlin Wall and the Cuban missile buildup.

Mobilizing the Masses

As to its specific content Nikita Khrushchev has said that

the policy of peaceful coexistence, as regards its social content, is a form of intense economic, political, and ideological struggle of the proletariat against the aggressive forces of imperialism in the international arena.

From this definition, it would appear that peaceful coexistence, inasmuch as it prescribes "intense struggle," does not accord with the meaning of the word "peaceful." But the *Statement of the 81 Communist and Workers Parties* of December 1960, a major policy declaration, goes into greater detail:

> The policy of peaceful coexistence is a policy of mobilizing the masses and launching vigorous action against the enemies of peace. Peaceful coexistence of states does not imply renunciation of the class struggle. . . . The coexistence of states with different social systems is a form of class struggle between socialism and capitalism. In conditions of peaceful coexistence favorable opportunities are provided for the development of the class struggle in the capitalist countries and the national-liberation movement of the peoples of the colonial and dependent countries. In their turn, the successes of the revolutionary class and national-liberation struggle promote peaceful coexistence. The Communists consider it their duty to fortify the faith of the people in the possibility of furthering peaceful coexistence, their determination to prevent world war. They will do their utmost for the people to weaken imperialism and limit its sphere of action by an active struggle for peace, democracy, and national liberation.

It should be noted that Communists consider peaceful coexistence and the "national liberation movement," the revolutionary movement in the underdeveloped countries, to be mutually reinforcing. The principal impact of this mutual reinforcement is the ability to "limit the sphere of action" of "imperialism." Accurately translated, this means that the successes of the Communists can be turned into an advantage by restricting the freedom of action of the Western countries, chiefly the United States. . . .

It is fairly safe to assume that the Communists do not desire a general war at this time. They fully realize that whatever benefits would accrue to them as the result of a war would be outweighed by the damage which they would suffer. Khrushchev, speaking on

August 19, 1963, stressed that "we Communists want to win this struggle with the least losses."

However, it is quite a different matter to assume that, because the Communists do not view war as a realistic instrument of policy at the present time, they will never employ it. It is also necessary to point out that the Communists have differentiated between the various types of wars, and have clearly delineated those which *are* acceptable and are to be *encouraged and assisted.* . . .

Seeking Victory over Capitalism

While it has become fashionable in the West to speak of "victory" in the cold war as "meaningless," the Communists persist in employing it as an official goal. Needless to say, they have a very real appreciation that "victory" by means of nuclear war would very probably be a victory in the true sense for no one; but to exclude a single method of achieving victory as an unrealistic instrument of policy does not signify that the entire concept of victory has been relinquished.

That Communists envision a genuine "victory" is demonstrated by the remarks of Khrushchev in July 1963 following the signing of the Nuclear Test Ban Treaty:

> Today the imperialists pretend to be brave, but only in words, whereas in reality they tremble before the world of growing and strengthening socialism. And let them tremble. So much the better for us.

> If everyone acted and thought in the Communist way then there would be no antagonistic classes and Communism would already be victorious everywhere. However, while there are still two systems, socialist and capitalist, each system has its own policy, its own course, and we cannot but take into account the fact that two systems exist. *A fight is in progress between these two systems, a life and death combat. But we Communists want to win this struggle with the least losses and there is no doubt whatsoever that we shall win.*

The recognition that two systems do *in fact* exist in the same world is given only grudgingly; and because there does exist in the world an alternative system to that of the Communists, the contest between them assumes, in Khrushchev's own words, the form of "a life and death combat." Peaceful coexistence fulfills the Communist objectives in this mortal combat by "insuring" that victory is accomplished with minimal losses.

It follows from this statement that the Communists are prepared to accept some losses in propelling the revolution forward, but nowhere is it made clear just what these losses could entail. Despite the possibility of such setbacks, however, Khrushchev emphasizes the certainty of triumph.

The specific function of peaceful coexistence is not, as we have found, the establishment of a mere period of relative calm on a worldwide scale. Rather, it is to provide conditions favorable for waging a many-pronged offensive at and within the non-Communist world. Above all, it creates a degree of flexibility hitherto unknown to the Communist movement, inasmuch as it allows for harnessing and utilizing the most disparate forces to the revolutionary cause. . . .

A Threat to the Free World

Faced with such a real and formidable opponent, the West must clarify and reaffirm the goals which it has so long sought to achieve. And if a just and lasting peace is foremost among those goals, then it will have to keep sight of that goal while steeling itself to meet even greater threats than those experienced in the past.

There can be little doubt about the goals which the Communists have set for themselves; they have been forthrightly stated on these pages by the Communists themselves, and were summarized by Khrushchev:

> Capitalism . . . wants to bury the Socialist system and we want—not only want but have dug—quite a deep hole, and shall exert efforts to dig this hole deeper and bury the capitalist system forever.

Whether there will continue to be room on the earth for the opposing systems of capitalism and Communism is a question which history alone will answer. For our part, we are willing to examine serious proposals for peace at any time; but "peace" on the basis of the Communist doctrine of "peaceful coexistence" is clearly an impossibility.

There is, however, a very real danger to the free world should it fail to judge accurately the intentions of the Communists. After some eight years of peaceful coexistence as the principal strategic line of the international Communist movement, we have no evidence that it seeks genuine peace with the rest of the world. Above all, it is clear that the Communists have not given up their long-range goal of world domination, and in the final analysis we must judge their motivations according to that goal. An intervening period of "peace" and relaxation, regardless of how inviting it may seem, must not be allowed to lower the guard of the free world.

A Great Paradox

It is clear that when Communists employ the language of "peace," they do so to mask their true strategic purpose: the isolation, encirclement, weakening, and final destruction of the free world and its way of life. The cold war has not concluded, but has entered a new and still more complex phase in which the spectrum of psychological, political, economic, and class warfare will be radically expanded. Such classic techniques as subversion, espionage, propaganda, sabotage, terrorism, deceit, and incited disorder will remain and be refined; but the new techniques of nuclear blackmail are also to be employed whenever feasible. It would be totally unrealistic to hold, as some do, that nuclear weapons have only a military purpose. Long ago the Soviet Union appreciated fully the political purposes of these enormously destructive modern weapons, and their early decisions to invest huge sums of money and manpower into their development indicates their willingness to attain real supremacy over the West.

During the period of peaceful coexistence, the Communists also hope to reap the benefits of a worldwide "détente," i.e., a relaxation of tensions. Under such conditions they would hope not only to gain through an American and Western slowdown in armaments, but also to subvert and paralyze hostile governments in the hope that at the critical moment such governments will capitulate or will be incapable of offering effective resistance.

The great paradox of our time may well turn out to be our inability to recognize that the cold war has in reality become more intense despite the increasing appearances of peace. It need not be emphasized that the overwhelming sentiment of the free world is to live in peace. But to mistake the illusion of peace for genuine peace would be a profoundly dangerous, perhaps fatal mistake.

Our purpose in this great struggle imposed upon us by the Communist world is, as our Presidents and statesmen have repeatedly stressed, the victory of our way of life. If the clash between the two systems is, as the Communists never tire of stating, irreconcilable, then our victory will not be achieved until freedom and justice prevail everywhere in the world.

Viewpoint 5

"'The war against Vietnam [could have been] irrevocably won in six weeks.'"

The United States Could Have Won the War in Vietnam

Steve Farrell

Although President John F. Kennedy supported the unstable democratic government of South Vietnam by sending military machinery and advisers, he would not intervene with troops when Communist North Vietnam threatened to take over the country. His successor, Lyndon Johnson, advocated stronger action. When, on August 4, 1964, North Vietnam launched what many claim was a dubious attack on American ships in the Gulf of Tonkin, Congress granted Johnson broad war powers to intervene in the region. Johnson responded with air attacks against North Vietnam. U.S. involvement in Vietnam escalated under Johnson, who introduced combat troops to Vietnam in March 1965. By 1967, 15,997 U.S. servicemen had been killed, and American opposition to the war grew.

Richard Nixon, who succeeded Johnson as president, expanded the war into neighboring Laos and Cambodia. When American college students protesting the invasions were killed, American opposition increased, and Nixon began to withdraw

Steve Farrell, "Why We Lost in Vietnam," *Spintech*, vol. 2, July 12, 1999. Copyright © 1999 by *Spintech*. Reproduced by permission.

troops from Vietnam. The Nixon administration engineered the Paris Peace Accord, ending open hostilities between the United States and North Vietnam in 1973. By this time, 47,359 U.S. soldiers had died. South Vietnamese forces tried to keep Communist forces at bay without U.S. assistance, but Saigon fell on April 30, 1975.

Since the fall of Saigon, analysts have debated whether or not the United States could have won the war in Vietnam. In the following viewpoint political columnist Steve Farrell claims that U.S. forces had all the tools needed to win the war and defeat Communist expansion in Vietnam. However, U.S. political leaders were not fighting communism, Farrell argues; they were supporting a policy of international cooperation—even with nations and leaders known to be tyrannical and oppressive. To achieve their objectives, Farrell maintains, U.S. leaders imposed "rules of engagement" that restricted the use of military tactics that could have resulted in a U.S. victory.

In 1985, actor Sylvester Stallone, starring for the second time as disillusioned Vietnam Vet and decorated fictional war hero John Rambo, gave us a film that was famously implausible for its action hero stunts—yet fabulously popular, and more importantly, bitingly astute concerning our loss in Vietnam.

His words were few, but his query, "Are we allowed to win this time?" received five stars from cheering veterans in the aisles of movie theatres who were just as anxious as Rambo to get another shot at victory—this time without one hand tied behind their back.

After viewing the film, one veteran told me with emotion, "For the first time I feel like I can hold my head high!"

As grossly animated a character as Rambo was, he did what the United States soldier could have done all along, if permitted, and that was send Communist Vietnam into the trash heap of history. But, as in Korea, so it was in Vietnam: a war fought in the name of internationalism would by design fail.

Many will dispute that point. Former State Department head Henry Kissinger argued that we lost because of our military's unfamiliarity with guerrilla warfare and by virtue of the divisive nature of our democratic government, which provided no staying power and thus no match for a patient communist enemy.

Others, like the Joint Chiefs of Staff in July of 1965, identified America's lack of a "will to win," as the problem. Historian Paul Johnson pinpointed "a unique succession of misjudgments, all made with the best intentions," as the indisputable cause.

Creating and Aiding the Enemy

But white-washing what happened in Vietnam as a succession of misjudgments reeks of the kind of Pollyanna-ism that has typified the Republican response to "mistakes" in US foreign policy dating back to a series of similar "misjudgments" with Hitler, Stalin, Mao, Castro, and later Ortega, Khomeini, Hussein, Aristide, and . . . Milosevic.[1] Amazingly, almost all of these henchmen were characterized kindly at one time to the American people as Uncle Joe's,[2] agrarian reformers, or as the George Washington's of their respective countries. And so we supported them with money and technology, and pulled the plug on supporting their pro-western opponents, even as piles of evidence indicated that none of the above deserved an ounce of trust.

But then, in the venture called internationalism creating and aiding the enemies you will later pretend to oppose appears strangely to be an accepted rule of the game.

Vietnam fit the pattern.

It was our "fervent anti-colonialist" Office of Strategic Services, predecessor of the CIA, which sponsored Communist leader Ho Chi Minh in his putsch, known as the August Revolution, which ousted the pro-French emperor of Vietnam.

A "misjudgment." And then when Ho Chi Minh began to do in Vietnam what we surely expect communists to do, he suddenly became our enemy. Could it be that a communist threat in In-

---

1. The leaders to whom the author refers are Adolf Hitler of Germany, Joseph Stalin of the Soviet Union, Mao Tse-tung of Communist China, Fidel Castro of Cuba, Daniel Ortega of Nicaragua, the Ayatollah Khomeini of Iran, Saddam Hussein of Iraq, Jean-Bertrand Aristide of Haiti, and Slobodan Milosevic of Yugoslavia.   2. "Uncle Joe" was a name given to Joseph Stalin to gain support for a U.S.-Soviet alliance needed to defeat Nazi Germany.

dochina, justifying the creation of another UN regional military alliance spreading internationalism's wings into stubborn, non-aligned Asia, was just what the doctor ordered? So it seemed.

An International Treaty

Thus in 1954, with the zealous support of Democratic President Harry Truman, the Southeast Asian Treaty Organization (SEATO) was formed as a sister organization to NATO.

In 1961 SEATO sprang to life when President John F. Kennedy—without congressional consent—sent troops to Vietnam "because the United States and our allies are committed by the SEATO treaty to act to meet the common danger of aggression in Southeast Asia."

And this we did, said State Department Bulletin 8062, with the blessing of the "UN Security Council." As the Bulletin further explained, for "the Southeast Asia Treaty Organization (SEATO) was designed as a collective defense arrangement under Article 51 of the UN Charter."

The Rules of Engagement

That should have been a clue that we were in for trouble in Vietnam. Enter the "Rules of Engagement." Co-authored by fellow internationalists and Council of Foreign Relations members Secretary of State Dean Rusk and Secretary of Defense Robert McNamara, these rules insured that we could not win and that the communists could not lose. Understandably, they were kept secret for 20 years.

It took a subpoena, and a lot of arm twisting from Senator Barry Goldwater, to finally have these "rules of engagement" hauled out of the State Department's vaults, declassified, and published in the Congressional Record, for all the world to see—a decade after the war was over.

The rules were startling.

Here are a few: U.S. pilots were forbidden to bomb Soviet made SAM missile sites under construction, but could risk their lives firing at them after they were fully operational. Pilots and ground forces were not allowed to destroy communist aircraft on the ground but only those armed and dangerous in the air. Truck depots 200 yards away from main roads were forbidden targets for American soldiers; but trucks on the road could be attacked. Pilots flying over supply ships laden with war materials on their way to North Vietnam's Haiphong Harbor were ordered to leave them alone, even as they carried the weapons which would kill Americans.

Throughout the war returning troops told of being ordered not to shoot until shot at, not to attack the enemy's "safe" areas, and not to hold terrain that had been won at considerable cost in lives and labor.

Ammunition "quotas," halted attacks and reversed victories, while paradoxically, vast quantities of ammunition were reportedly fired at "undefined targets."

Topping off this series of "misjudgments" President Lyndon B. Johnson, the Commander-In-Chief, authorized the sale of US "non-military" hardware to the East European communist block nations who unsurprisingly converted the same into military hardware, which was shipped to North Vietnam sporting labels "made in the USA."

Those partially made-in-the-USA weapons killed American boys.

Congressman H.R. Gross (R-IA), described all of this as "a betrayal to international politics and intrigue."

Fighting for the Wrong Reason

Which is the point. This was the second US involved war officially fought in the name of the International Order, supposedly to check communism, but which by design preserved communism and made America look like a fool.

But this is wrong. To be precise, the embarrassment should be placed at the doorstep of the United Nations and the host of internationalists in this country and abroad who support its institutions and philosophies. Vietnam was a war fought in favor of the international order, not a war fought to further the interests of anti-communism and US nationalism.

Had it been a traditional American war, things would have been different.

"The war against Vietnam [could have been] irrevocably won in six weeks," was the collective opinion of a prestigious panel of former and current Joint Chief of Staffs, Chief of Staffs, and generals, interviewed in the March 1968 issue of *Science & Mechanics.*

But it wasn't, and instead, they said we chose to fight "a war in a weak-sister manner that is unprecedented throughout the history of military science."

In the end, like Korea, Vietnam fell into the hands of the communists, 48,000 Americans died, another 300,000 were wounded, 1.2 million Vietnamese perished (the rest were enslaved), and dominoes would follow in Indochina.

Our last "misjudgment" in Vietnam was to recommend a familiar UN "democracy/unifying/peace" strategy, a coalition government combining North and South Vietnam. Unity resulted all right—Communist style.

Audaciously internationalists never acknowledged their part in this fiasco, but have rather used Vietnam to condemn nationalism, to cite the no-win predicament of guerrilla warfare as additional proof that war should be outlawed and nations disarmed, and to suggest in the future that the UN and its surrogates should intervene earlier—even before "threatening" nations attack.

Viewpoint 6

"In May 1964, [President Lyndon] Johnson was convinced that Vietnam was not worth fighting for and that we could not win a war in Southeast Asia."

The United States Could Not Have Won the War in Vietnam

Regis T. Sabol

President John F. Kennedy supported the democratic government of South Vietnam by sending military equipment and advisers, but he would not send American troops when Communist North Vietnam threatened to take over the country. His successor, Lyndon Johnson, advocated stronger action. When on August 4, 1964, North Vietnam launched what many claim was a dubious attack on American ships in the Gulf of Tonkin, Johnson responded with air attacks against North Vietnam. The war escalated under Johnson, who introduced combat troops to Vietnam in March 1965. By 1967, 15,997 U.S. servicemen had been killed in the war, and opposition to the war grew, dividing the nation. Richard Nixon, who succeeded Johnson as president, expanded the war into neighboring Laos and Cambodia. When American college students protesting the invasions were killed, American opposition increased, pressuring Nixon to end U.S. involvement. The Nixon administration engineered the Paris Peace Accord, ending open hostilities between the United States and North Vietnam in 1973. By this time, 47,359 U.S. soldiers had died as a result of the hostilities, and 2,338 were missing in action. South Vietnamese forces tried to keep Communist forces at bay without U.S assistance, but Saigon, the capital of South Vietnam, fell on April 30, 1975.

Regis T. Sabol, editor of *A New Deal*, an online magazine of political commentary, argues in the following viewpoint that military and political leaders knew early on that the war could not be won. According to Sabol, a full-scale military attack on North Vietnam would have provoked direct Chinese involvement, possibly triggering World War III. The United States was not willing to run that risk, but without a full-scale attack on North Vietnam, American victory was impossible.

The Vietnam War. You know, it's a funny thing. I don't mean in the sense that it was hilarious. Quite the contrary. A war that cost more than 58,000 American lives and roughly eight million Vietnamese lives is certainly no laughing matter. Yet, a quarter century after its ignominious end, we Americans are still arguing about it. Indeed, based on my experience, it appears that many Americans, if not most Americans, are unwilling to accept the obvious realities of that horrendous experience.

And what are these obvious realities? 1. We had no business being in Vietnam because, essentially it was another country's civil war; 2. We violated the Geneva Accords[1] by injecting ourselves into that war; and, 3., and most importantly, we threw away 58,000 American lives in a war our national leaders knew from the outset we could not win. Transcripts of Lyndon Johnson's secretly

1. An international conference was held in Geneva, Switzerland, to settle the war France had been waging against Communist forces in Vietnam. The Geneva Accords stated that Vietnam was to become an independent nation. Elections were to be held in July 1956, under international supervision. During the two-year interval until the elections, the country would be split into two parts—the North and the South.

recorded audio tapes reveal that in May 1964, Johnson was convinced that Vietnam was not worth fighting for and that we could not win a war in Southeast Asia.

Examining the Evidence

While many Americans who don't know the contents of these transcripts may reject my observations about the Vietnam War, many historians, other scholars, and, most importantly, key players in the war side with me. The most recent evidence comes from Robert S. McNamara's *Argument Without End: In Search of Answers to the Vietnam Tragedy*. The book, co-authored by James Blight, Robert Brigham, Thomas Biersteker, and Herbert Schandler, gives an account of and the conclusions reached by American and Vietnamese experts on the war, by way of being principal decision makers in the conduct of the war and scholars who have studied the war extensively.

These two groups met seven times over a four-year period to answer four questions: 1. If each side had known the truth about the other's reality, might the outcome have been less tragic? 2. Were there missed opportunities to avoid the conflict? 3. Could the war have ended much sooner than it did? 4. Could the United States have achieved a military victory in Vietnam? The answers to these questions are yes, yes, yes, and no.

McNamara, you may recall, was pilloried for confessing in an earlier memoir, *In Retrospect: The Tragedy and Lessons of Vietnam*, that, as secretary of defense in the Kennedy and Johnson administrations, he had been dead wrong in thinking that the war was necessary and winnable. Conservatives and former government officials in the Kennedy, Johnson, and Nixon administrations, as well as many Vietnam veterans, accused him of being a traitor by demeaning what they still believe was a noble cause. They viewed McNamara's recanting of his support for the war as nothing less than apostasy. I suspect none of them stopped to think about the validity of their views on the Vietnam War.

The Ghost of Vietnam

Sen. John McCain's failed run for the Republican presidential nomination [in 2000] revealed just how strongly many Americans still believe it was a just war worth fighting. They further believe that "by standing up to the Communists" in Vietnam, we halted Communist aggression throughout the rest of Southeast Asia. The tenacity with which supporters of the war hold onto this belief reveals the depth of their ignorance about Vietnamese history and the fervent nationalism that inspired the Vietnamese to defeat the Japanese, the French, and the Americans in order to achieve independence.

Although Sen. McCain focused on campaign finance reform, his real drawing card was as a prisoner of war for six years at the notorious Hanoi Hilton.[2] At every campaign stop, admirers thrust copies of McCain's autobiography in front of him for an autograph. It seems as if McCain's ordeal as a prisoner of war, which he describes in frightening detail, is evidence that the North Vietnamese were, in fact, the barbaric monsters they were portrayed as during the war.

While I do not condone the inhumane treatment the Vietnamese inflicted on American prisoners of war, we have to understand how the Vietnamese felt about the attacks on their cities. Let's put it this way: How would we have felt if, during the Civil War, the British supported the South and sent an expeditionary force to fight against the North. In this scenario, the British navy, masters of the seas at that time, bombarded eastern cities such as New York and Boston? How would you feel about those Englishmen lobbing shells at your home, killing your friends and relatives? To the Vietnamese, we were interlopers, brutally attacking their country without just cause. They believed we were out to destroy and conquer them. . . .

The Truth Is Out There

Argument Without End confirms that the Vietnam War was, in fact, a ghastly, foolhardy political and military blunder of monstrous proportions. McNamara is right to call the Vietnam War a tragedy, especially since, as *Argument Without End* demonstrates beyond a shadow of any reasonable doubt, the war was avoidable and un-

2. The Hanoi Hilton refers to Hoa Lo prison in Hanoi, which was the most famous institution in the North Vietnamese prison system.

necessary. Ironically, many of the conclusions of the American-Vietnamese joint study of the war were not unexpected revelations.

Long before McNamara published his first *mea culpa* in 1995, Frances FitzGerald's *Fire in the Lake: The Vietnamese and the Americans in Vietnam*, published in 1972 as U.S. involvement in the war was winding down; Stanley Karnow's *Vietnam: A History*, published in 1983 as a companion to the PBS television series; and Neil Sheehan's *A Bright Shining Lie: John Paul Vann and America*

Doonesbury. © 1970 by Garry Trudeau. Reprinted with permission.

in Vietnam, published in 1988, all documented the folly that led America into the quagmire and defeat in Southeast Asia. So did a number of other books, many of them by Vietnam veterans and journalists who were "on the ground" during the war. In addition, several documentary series that air regularly on such cable outlets as A&E, the Discovery channel, and the History channel point to the same conclusion.

Yet I found myself recently arguing with a young man and a young woman barely over twenty-one who wholeheartedly believed our cause in Vietnam was righteous, and that I was a traitor for expressing my belief that the Vietnam War was a horrendous mistake. Nor was this the only occasion in which young people with no actual memory of the war have castigated me for my opposition to it. Several have proudly declared they would have unhesitatingly fought in Vietnam, had they been old enough to do so.

Perhaps this simplistic view of America's involvement in Vietnam is a tribute of sorts to the power of media saturation. *The Green Berets* is, hands down, the worst movie about the Vietnam War ever made. It is also the most popular movie macho screen idol John Wayne ever made. Ted Turner's two cable channels run *The Green Berets* every few months, and American Movie Classics, another cable outlet, also shows it periodically. I've been in bars when *The Green Berets* is on TV. Patrons, usually males, watch the movie as intently as if it were the Super Bowl, even though they have probably seen it countless times.

Then there are the "Chuck Norris saving American prisoners of war from their evil Commie North Vietnamese captors" flicks that also appear regularly on several cable outlets. These bad movies seem to have had a more profound influence on how we view the Vietnam War than did such brilliant films as *Apocalypse Now* and *Platoon*, the latter an Oscar winner for best picture of the year.

That *The Green Berets* presents a wildly distorted view of the war is apparently irrelevant. That is the picture of the war too many Americans accept. Despite all evidence to the contrary, these latter-day champions of the war have bought into the revisionist notion that the only reasons we lost the war were politicians who would not unleash the full might of the American military and the news media who distorted the military's achievements that would lead to victory. These views have gained such currency that they need to be examined and refuted.

Blaming the Politicians

First, let's look at the argument that the military had to fight the war with one hand tied behind their backs. It is true that American pilots were prohibited from attacking Soviet and Chinese vessels unloading missiles, weapons, and other war material from the docks at Haiphong or from bombing military installations that may have been manned by Soviet or Chinese advisors.

What critics of this micromanagement ignore is the reason Lyndon Johnson declared those targets off-limits. Quite simply, Johnson did not want Vietnam to escalate into World War III. Considering the precariousness of our relations with the Soviet Union and with China at the time, this was a reasonable fear.

We all know, of course, that Barry Goldwater promised to "bomb them into the Stone Age" if elected president in 1964. And there are those who now believe Goldwater was right; we should have bombed them into the Stone Age. The harsh reality is that, even if we would have done so, we could not have won that war. What would we have done next? Invaded the North? That would have mired us even more deeply in a protracted guerrilla war that would have gone on for decades, a war we most assuredly could not have won.

Even more frighteningly, *Argument Without End* reveals that invading North Vietnam would have triggered China's entry into the war, just as Douglas MacArthur's foolhardy march to the Yalu brought China into the Korean War, with disastrous results. What other military alternative was available to us? Nuclear weapons? That surely would have invited global nuclear catastrophe. As McNamara, among others, eventually concluded, military victory was impossible.

Blaming the Media

The belief that the news media lost the war still lingers among diehard Vietnam hawks, right-wing radio talk show hosts such as Rush Limbaugh, and young people whose only knowledge of the war comes from the likes of Limbaugh and his ilk. Blaming *The*

New York Times or Walter Cronkite for losing the war is akin to blaming the wicked messenger.

Ironically, most American print and electronic media, including *The Times*, supported the Kennedy and Johnson administrations' Vietnam policies throughout the early years of the war. For example, every major newspaper and magazine endorsed the Gulf of Tonkin Resolution in August 1964, that gave Johnson *carte blanche* to make Vietnam an American war that would eventually put 500,000 American troops on the ground in Vietnam.

(You may recall that Congress passed the Gulf of Tonkin resolution after two alleged attacks on U.S. warships in international waters. Evidence released by the Pentagon and eventually confirmed by the Vietnamese revealed that the second "attack" never occurred. The single action by Vietnamese gun boats was in response to an incursion into Vietnamese waters by a U.S. Naval warship acting in support of a sabotage mission.)

It was not until 1966, when the futility of our involvement in Vietnam became apparent to a relatively small group of journalists, that media criticism of the war began to surface. Even then, most American media continued their unequivocal support of the war. That support did not waver, even through the Nixon years.

Still, the news media remain a favorite scapegoat for why we lost the war in Vietnam. The most vocal proponent of this view is retired Gen. William Westmoreland, the American commander in Vietnam during much of the war. Westmoreland's critics occasionally referred to him as Gen. Waste More Land because of his profligate use of napalm, Agent Orange, and other weapons that irrevocably damaged the Vietnamese ecosystem.

Light at the End of the Tunnel?

To this day, Westmoreland blames the media for his defeat in Vietnam. Westmoreland points in particular to the 1968 Tet offensive, a battle most observers agree was the turning point in the war. Westmoreland insists we won Tet because we killed far more of theirs than they killed of ours. He continues to call it a great victory and blames the media for portraying Tet as a major defeat for American policy.

What Westmoreland conveniently forgets is that less than two months before Tet, he loudly proclaimed before a joint session of Congress that he "could see the light at the end of the tunnel" in Vietnam. Victory was at hand, he confidently told the American people. Westmoreland's "light at the end of the tunnel" turned out to be the explosive nation-wide violence of the Tet offensive, for which he and his commanders were totally unprepared. Little wonder that Walter Cronkite, the most trusted voice in broadcast journalism at the time, concluded that it was time for us to get out of Vietnam.

After years of protracted negotiations, we were finally able to extricate ourselves from Vietnam in 1973 by agreeing to terms that we had rejected in 1968 and for almost every year after that. In the meantime, roughly 30,000 American servicemen died for no other reason than to insure that Richard Nixon, who promised Americans in 1968 that he had a secret plan to end the war, would be re-elected to a second term. Nixon, of course, would resign in disgrace in 1975, the same year North Vietnamese tanks rolled into Saigon, unifying Vietnam and achieving their sole purpose in fighting the war.

They're Still "Gooks"

As it turned out, South Vietnam was no "domino" in a grand monolithic communist strategy to conquer all of Southeast Asia. In fact, it wasn't long before Vietnamese troops were fighting first the Chinese on their border, and then the Communist Khmer Rouge in Cambodia. So much for dominoes.

We now have full diplomatic relations with Vietnam, which offers a source of cheap labor and a market for American products. American corporations are trampling over one another to establish lucrative markets in the land of our former enemy. The Vietnamese government is wired to Microsoft technology, and Vietnamese kids drink Coca-Cola, wear Michael Jordan basketball shirts, and dance to American rock music.

And yet the shadow of the Vietnam War still hangs over us like a nightmare that won't go away. Veterans' groups continue to demand that the Vietnamese give a full accounting of our servicemen missing in action, as if the Vietnamese have hostage Americans squirreled away in some jungle camp. Several Chuck Norris movies propagated this very fantasy, with Chuck, of course, rescuing them from their slant-eyed captors.

Some Americans simply refuse to accept that these men aren't missing and need only be found alive in some Vietnamese prison camp. That's not going to happen. Ever. They're dead. They were blown out of the sky or blown to bits by mortar or artillery. The Vietnamese have, in fact, gone out of their way to help recover the remains of missing U.S. servicemen. That doesn't matter to the thousands of Americans who display bumper stickers and flags demanding a return of our prisoners of war. When Sen. McCain referred to his former captors as "gooks," most Americans didn't bat an eye at the blatant racism of his comment. The unspoken truth is most Americans agree with McCain. To them, as well as to McCain, they're still gooks.

How ironic that after the most catastrophic war in human history, we were able to forgive the Germans and the Japanese for the unspeakable atrocities they committed during World War II. Yet, to many Americans, the Vietnamese will always be gooks.

CHAPTER 3

From Détente to the Cold War's End

Chapter Preface

During the Cold War, U.S. leaders often spoke of the United States as the leader of the Free World, its role to protect nations from Communist oppression and make the world safe for democracy and freedom. This perception of America's role had deep roots. When the United States declared its independence from England in 1776 and established a new form of government—which expanded the scope of individual freedom—Americans saw themselves as champions of a new world. Foreign policy scholar Itai Sneh explains how this vision has long shaped American policies: "Their self-perception as role models for the rest of humanity behooved Americans to conduct a foreign policy that espoused tolerance and self-reliance and that accorded protection to the weak from the abuse of power through observance of the fundamental principles of human rights." Cold War policy, in particular, was often sold to the American people as a natural extension of America's long commitment to human rights. At the same time, American leaders portrayed the Soviet system as the natural enemy of freedom and justice.

It was not surprising, then, that when Americans discovered in the late 1970s that in its effort to prevent the rise of Communist-leaning governments in developing nations, the U.S. government had supported corrupt, despotic leaders known to abuse the human rights of its citizens, many Americans became disillusioned. According to historian Robert J. Allison, "Critics at home charged that U.S. campaigns to prevent Soviet domination in Asia, Europe, and Africa were mere covers for the protection of right-wing dictators. Were Francisco Franco of Spain, Mohammad Reza Pahlevi of Iran, Augusto Pinochet Ugarte of Chile, Ngo Dinh Diem of Vietnam, or the white government of South Africa preferable to socialist government?" Many critics charged that the United States was so blindly intent on containing communism and its perceived abuses that it supported regimes that perpetuated the very human rights violations the policies were designed to prevent.

President Jimmy Carter, elected in this distrustful environment, pledged to pursue human rights, and, writes Allison, "to redirect American energies to a higher purpose than protecting favored regimes." Carter's secretary of state, Cyrus R. Vance, articulated Carter's vision this way: "Historically, our country had been a force for progress in human affairs. A nation that saw itself as a 'beacon on the hill' for the rest of mankind could not content itself with power politics alone. It could not properly ignore the growing demands of individuals around the world for the fulfillment of their rights." In pursuit of its human rights agenda, the Carter administration censured, reduced aid to, and imposed sanctions against Cold War allies that abused human rights, including nations such as Argentina, Chile, Iran, and Nicaragua. Historian Paul DuQuenoy maintains, "Several pro-American governments became more stable and less heinous because their relations with the United States had to accommodate human-rights considerations."

Not everyone has praised Carter's policies, however. Opponents claim that in trying to strike a balance between protecting human rights and preserving America's political and economic interests, Carter often implemented his human rights policies inconsistently. According to historian Robert E. Williams, "In addition to being advanced with rhetoric that often sounded self-righteous and arrogant, the Carter administration's human-rights policy appeared selective." For example, during the Carter administration the United States was trying to establish diplomatic and economic relations with China for the first time since China had become a Communist nation; thus Carter ignored China's egregious human rights violations and the oppressive regimes of its satellites, such as the Pol Pot regime in Cambodia, perpetrator of one of the worst genocides in history. U.S. relations with the Soviet Union, on the other hand, had already begun to warm during a period of détente; thus Carter felt safer applying pressure on the Soviet Union to improve its human rights record. For many, this inconsistency was unconscionable.

Other critics contend that Carter's Cold War human rights programs were counterproductive. They claim that U.S. pressure to end human rights violations among its allies ultimately damaged U.S. interests by leading to catastrophic regime changes in those nations. Critics often cite Iran, the closest U.S. ally in the Persian Gulf, as an example of this problem. The dismal state of human-rights in Iran was well known but ignored by the Nixon administration, which wanted to maintain good relations with this strategic ally—one of the few nations in the Persian Gulf that was friendly to the United States. In contrast, the Carter administration publicly denounced the shah of Iran's human rights violations and cut U.S. foreign aid and military assistance to that country. The shah's regime eventually fell to the opposition, which was hostile to the United States. The overthrow of the shah and the installment of the repressive regime of Ayatollah Khomieni, who denounced the United States, concludes historian Robert E. Williams, "resulted in the loss of a strategically situated ally."

Whether promoting human rights was a beneficial Cold War policy remains the subject of debate. In the following chapter political decision makers and commentators explore the effectiveness of other policies employed by the United States as well as those implemented by the Soviet Union during the 1970s until the end of the Cold War.

Viewpoint 1

"There can be no peaceful international order without a constructive relationship between the United States and the Soviet Union."

Détente Is a Constructive U.S. Policy

Henry A. Kissinger

Henry A. Kissinger was U.S. secretary of state from 1973 to 1977; he played a major role in formulating American foreign policy during this period. Kissinger established a policy of détente, a relaxation of tensions with the Soviet Union, and pursued the normalization of relations with China. Kissinger also helped initiate the Strategic Arms Limitation Talks.

In the following viewpoint, taken from testimony given before the Senate Foreign Relations Committee in September 1974, Kissinger explains the purposes and accomplishments of détente. According to Kissinger, the threat of nuclear war makes it imperative that the United States and Soviet Union work together to reduce the tensions between them. He argues that the United States should discontinue efforts to contain and defeat the Soviet Union and work toward achieving mutual goals such as ending the arms race.

Henry A. Kissinger, testimony before the Senate Foreign Relations Committee, Washington, DC, September 1974.

Since the dawn of the nuclear age the world's fears of holocaust and its hopes for peace have turned on the relationship between the United States and the Soviet Union. . . .

Understanding the Differences

The destructiveness of modern weapons defines the necessity of the task; deep differences in philosophy and interests between the United States and the Soviet Union point up its difficulty. These differences do not spring from misunderstanding or personalities or transitory factors:

- They are rooted in history and in the way the two countries have developed.
- They are nourished by conflicting values and opposing ideologies.
- They are expressed in diverging national interests that produce political and military competition.
- They are influenced by allies and friends whose association we value and whose interests we will not sacrifice.

Paradox confuses our perception of the problem of peaceful coexistence: if peace is pursued to the exclusion of any other goal, other values will be compromised and perhaps lost; but if unconstrained rivalry leads to nuclear conflict, these values, along with everything else, will be destroyed in the resulting holocaust. However competitive they may be at some levels of their relationship, both major nuclear powers must base their policies on the premise that neither can expect to impose its will on the other without running an intolerable risk. The challenge of our time is to reconcile the reality of competition with the imperative of coexistence.

There can be no peaceful international order without a constructive relationship between the United States and the Soviet Union. There will be no international stability unless both the Soviet Union and the United States conduct themselves with restraint and unless they use their enormous power for the benefit of mankind.

The Policy of Détente

Thus we must be clear at the outset on what the term "détente" entails. It is the search for a more constructive relationship with the Soviet Union reflecting the realities I have outlined. It is a continuing process, not a final condition that has been or can be realized at any one specific point in time. And it has been pursued by successive American leaders, though the means have varied as have world conditions.

Some fundamental principles guide this policy:

- The United States cannot base its policy solely on Moscow's good intentions. But neither can we insist that all forward movement must await a convergence of American and Soviet purposes. We seek, regardless of Soviet intentions, to serve peace through a systematic resistance to pressure and conciliatory responses to moderate behavior.

- We must oppose aggressive actions and irresponsible behavior. But we must not seek confrontations lightly.

- We must maintain a strong national defense while recognizing that in the nuclear age the relationship between military strength and politically usable power is the most complex in all history.

- Where the age-old antagonism between freedom and tyranny is concerned, we are not neutral. But other imperatives impose limits on our ability to produce internal changes in foreign countries. Consciousness of our limits is recognition of the necessity of peace—not moral callousness. The preservation of human life and human society are moral values, too.

- We must be mature enough to recognize that to be stable a relationship must provide advantages to both sides and that the most constructive international relationship are those in which both parties perceive an element of gain. Moscow will benefit from certain measures, just as we will from others. The balance cannot be struck on each issue every day, but only over the whole range of relations and over a period of time. . . .

An Uneven Course

The course of détente has not been smooth or even. As late as 1969, Soviet-American relations were ambiguous and uncertain. To be sure, negotiations on Berlin and SALT [Strategic Arms Limitation Talks] had begun. But the tendency toward confrontation appeared dominant.

We were challenged by Soviet conduct in the Middle East cease-fire of August 1970, during the Syrian invasion of Jordan in September 1970, on the question of a possible Soviet submarine base in Cuba, in actions around Berlin, and during the Indo-Pakistani war. Soviet policy seemed directed toward fashioning a détente in bilateral relations with our Western European allies, while challenging the United States.

We demonstrated then, and stand ready to do so again, that America will not yield to pressure or the threat of force. We made clear then, as we do today, that détente cannot be pursued selectively in one area or toward one group of countries only. For us détente is indivisible.

Finally, a breakthrough was made in 1971 on several fronts—in the Berlin settlement, in the SALT talks, in other arms control negotiations—that generated the process of détente. It consists of these elements: An elaboration of principles; political discussions to solve outstanding issues and to reach cooperative agreements; economic relations; and arms control negotiations, particularly those concerning strategic arms. . . .

A Strategic Relationship

We cannot expect to relax international tensions or achieve a more stable international system should the two strongest nuclear powers conduct an unrestrained strategic arms race. Thus, perhaps the single most important component of our policy toward the Soviet Union is the effort to limit strategic weapons competition.

The competition in which we now find ourselves is historically unique:

- Each side has the capacity to destroy civilization as we know it.
- Failure to maintain equivalence could jeopardize not only our freedom but our very survival.
- The lead time for technological innovation is so long, yet the pace of change so relentless, that the arms race and strategic policy itself are in danger of being driven by technological necessity.
- When nuclear arsenals reach levels involving thousands of launchers and over 10,000 warheads, and when the characteristics of the weapons of the two sides are so incommensurable,

it becomes difficult to determine what combination of numbers of strategic weapons and performance capabilities would give one side a militarily and politically useful superiority. At a minimum, clear changes in the strategic balance can be achieved only by efforts so enormous and by increments so large that the very attempt would be highly destabilizing.

• The prospect of a decisive military advantage, even if theoretically possible, is politically intolerable; neither side will passively permit a massive shift in the nuclear balance. Therefore the probable outcome of each succeeding round of competition is the restoration of a strategic equilibrium, but at increasingly higher levels of forces.

• The arms race is driven by political as well as military factors. While a decisive advantage is hard to calculate, the *appearance* of inferiority—whatever its actual significance—can have serious political consequences. With weapons that are unlikely to be used and for which there is no operational experience, the psychological impact can be crucial. Thus each side has a high incentive to achieve not only the reality but the appearance of equality. In a very real sense each side shapes the military establishment of the other.

If we are driven to it, the United States will sustain an arms race. Indeed, it is likely that the United States would emerge from such a competition with an edge over the Soviet Union in most significant categories of strategic arms. But the political or military benefit which would flow from such a situation would remain elusive. Indeed, after such an evolution it might well be that *both* sides would be worse off than before the race began. The enormous destructiveness of weapons and the uncertainties regarding their effects combine to make the massive use of such weapons increasingly incredible. . . .

Maintaining American Interests

To be sure, the process of détente raises serious issues for many people. Let me deal with these in terms of the principles which underlie our policy.

First, if détente is to endure, both sides must benefit. There is no question that the Soviet Union obtains benefits from détente.

On what other grounds would the tough-minded members of the Politburo sustain it? But the essential point surely must be that détente serves American and world interests as well.

If these coincide with some Soviet interests, this will only strengthen the durability of the process. . . .

Second, building a new relationship with the Soviet Union does not entail any devaluation of traditional alliance relations.

Our approach to relations with the U.S.S.R. has always been, and will continue to be, rooted in the belief that the cohesion of our alliances, and particularly the Atlantic alliance, is a precondition to establishing a more constructive relationship with the U.S.S.R.

Crucial, indeed unique, as may be our concern with Soviet power, we do not delude ourselves that we should deal with it alone. When we speak of Europe and Japan as representing centers of power and influence, we describe not merely an observable fact but an indispensable element in the equilibrium needed to keep the world at peace. The cooperation and partnership between us transcend formal agreements; they reflect values and traditions not soon, if ever, to be shared with our adversaries. . . .

Third, the emergence of more normal relations with the Soviet Union must not undermine our resolve to maintain our national defense.

There is a tendency in democratic societies to relax as dangers seem to recede; there is an inclination to view the maintenance of strength as incompatible with relaxation of tensions rather than its precondition. But this is primarily a question of leadership. We shall attempt to be vigilant to the dangers facing America. This administration will not be misled—or mislead—on issues of national defense. At the same time, we do not accept the proposition that we need crises to sustain our defense. A society that needs artificial crises to do what is needed for survival will soon find itself in mortal danger.

Fourth, we must know what can and cannot be achieved in changing human conditions in the East.

The question of dealing with Communist governments has troubled the American people and the Congress since 1917. There has always been a fear that by working with a government whose internal policies differ so sharply with our own we are in some manner condoning these policies or encouraging their continuation. Some argue that until there is a genuine "liberalization"—or signs of serious progress in this direction—all elements of conciliation in Soviet policy must be regarded as temporary and tactical. In that view, demands for internal changes must be the precondition for the pursuit of a relaxation of tensions with the Soviet Union.

Our view is different. We shall insist on responsible international behavior by the Soviet Union and use it as the primary index of our relationship. Beyond this we will use our influence to the maximum to alleviate suffering and to respond to humane appeals. We know what we stand for, and we shall leave no doubt about it. . . .

Encouraging Change

We have accomplished much. But we cannot demand that the Soviet Union, in effect, suddenly reverse five decades of Soviet, and centuries of Russian, history. Such an attempt would be futile and at the same time hazard all that has already been achieved. Changes in Soviet society have already occurred, and more will come. But they are most likely to develop through an evolution that can best go forward in an environment of decreasing international tensions. A renewal of the cold war will hardly encourage the Soviet Union to change its emigration policies or adopt a more benevolent attitude toward dissent.

Détente is a process, not a permanent achievement. The agenda is full and continuing. Obviously the main concern must be to reduce the sources of potential conflict. This requires efforts in several interrelated areas:

- The military competition in all its aspects must be subject to increasingly firm restraints by both sides.
- Political competition, especially in moments of crisis, must be guided by the principles of restraint set forth in the documents described earlier. Crises there will be, but the United States and the Soviet Union have a special obligation deriving from the unimaginable military power that they wield and represent. Exploitation of crisis situations for unilateral gain is not acceptable.

- Restraint in crises must be augmented by cooperation in removing the causes of crises. There have been too many instances, notably in the Middle East, which demonstrate that policies of unilateral advantage sooner or later run out of control and lead to the brink of war, if not beyond.
- The process of negotiations and consultation must be continuous and intense. But no agreement between the nuclear superpowers can be durable if made over the heads of other nations which have a stake in the outcome. We should not seek to impose peace; we can, however, see that our own actions and conduct are conducive to peace. . . .

We have insisted toward the Soviet Union that we cannot have the atmosphere of détente without the substance. It is equally clear that the substance of détente will disappear in an atmosphere of hostility.

We have profound differences with the Soviet Union—in our values, our methods, our vision of the future. But it is these very differences which compel any responsible administration to make a major effort to create a more constructive relationship.

We face an opportunity that was not possible twenty-five years, or even a decade, ago. If that opportunity is lost, its moment will not quickly come again. Indeed, it may not come at all.

As President [John F.] Kennedy pointed out: "For in the final analysis our most basic common link is that we all inhabit this small planet. We all breathe the same air. We all cherish our children's future. And we are all mortal."

Viewpoint 2

"Détente amounts to giving [U.S.] assets away without requiring any strategic benefits in return."

Détente Is a Flawed U.S. Policy

G. Warren Nutter

Henry Kissinger's policy of détente, the easing of tensions between the United States and the Soviet Union, was controversial during the 1970s. Opponents of détente, such as G. Warren Nutter, assistant secretary of defense for international security from 1969 to 1973, argued that the Soviet Union remained a dangerous adversary and that détente was only making it more dangerous. In the following viewpoint, excerpted from his book *Kissinger's Grand Design*, Nutter claims that détente has weakened U.S. power and strengthened the Soviet Union. According to Nutter, while the United States has reduced military spending in an effort to curb the arms race, the Soviet Union has used the opportunity to increase its military might. In addition, he asserts, arms reduction agreements between the two superpowers will not ensure peace. Rather than appease the Soviet Union, the United States must recognize that nation as an enemy, Nutter contends. Both before and after his government service, Nutter was a professor of economics at the University of Virginia at Charlottesville.

G. Warren Nutter, *Kissinger's Grand Design*. Washington, DC: American Enterprise Institute for Public Policy Research, 1975. Copyright © 1975 by American Enterprise Institute for Foreign Policy Research. Reproduced by permission.

S ecretary of State Henry A. Kissinger has implicitly renounced
his earlier conviction that only the exercise of power can check
Soviet strife with the Western world and that, unless Soviet weakness is exploited, deténte will merely hasten Soviet hegemony by
demoralizing the West. "Détente is an imperative," he now says.
"In a world shadowed by the danger of nuclear holocaust, there
is no rational alternative to the pursuit of relaxation of tensions."
That is, avoidance of the *risk* of war must be the supreme and
overriding goal of U.S. policy, almost regardless of cost in other
respects. . . .

One can only speculate on what caused such a profound change
in outlook. A case can be made that Kissinger simply saw no other
way to turn as he watched the tide of history sweep away, one by
one, the elements he had identified as essential for establishing an
international order. . . .

The Elements of Détente

There remains the question . . . of whether the substance of détente constitutes the best foreign policy for the United States. For
brevity, we shall use "détente" to mean the already described con-
figuration of policies and procedures specifically associated with
Kissinger's stewardship of foreign affairs, not the relaxation of international tensions in the abstract. The issue is whether détente,
so defined, is the best way to preserve the security of the West.

Détente involves a mixed strategy: interdependency is the car-
rot, deterrence the stick, and arms control the rein. Let us examine the relative importance of these elements, their mutual con-
sistency, and the compatibility of this strategy with the attainment
of peace and tranquillity.

Deterrence is obviously the key element, for without it security
of the West would depend solely on Soviet goodwill and self-
restraint, scarcely a strong reed to lean upon in the light of Soviet
history and ideology. By definition, effective arms control would
reduce the level of Western military strength required for deterrence, but the relation between deterrence and interdependency
is far more complex. Greater gains from so-called interdependency
might, by enhancing the Soviet stake in the existing international
order, provide an incentive to the Soviet Union to restrain its ex-

pansionist instinct. But the unilateral concessions yielding those gains will cause us to appear all the more weak-willed in the eyes of Soviet leaders, while the gains themselves increase Soviet power commensurately. Soviet leaders will consequently be tempted to seek even greater gains through power politics and to treat the United States as a weakling deserving contempt. Meanwhile, the atmosphere of détente is certain, as we now witness, to sway Western psychology toward downgrading the Soviet threat, cutting defense budgets, and disrupting alliances, the effect being a further tipping of the power balance in the Soviet Union's favor. The dynamics of this process can, as Kissinger once constantly warned, lead to demoralization of the West and Soviet victory by default.

Questioning Kissinger's Thesis

Kissinger's grand design rests on the thesis that the dominating effect of greater interdependency will be to restrain Soviet behavior, but he has little backing from history. Economic interdependence is scarcely new: on the eve of World War I, Norman Angell argued in *The Great Illusion* that the intricate network of world commerce had destroyed all possibility of gain from war. Yet the warring nations of Europe in the twentieth century, as in the nineteenth, normally were close trading partners. As Professor Gregory Grossman reminds us, "history provides little reassurance that trade ensures peace, and Russia's own history least of all. Germany was her largest trading partner just before each of the two World Wars, while China was her largest trading partner (and Russia China's) before the break between Moscow and Peking around 1960."

It is doubtful in any case that the interdependency seemingly envisaged by Kissinger can grow out of normal trading relations, since there is no reason to believe that the Soviet Union is about to abandon its traditional policy of autarky. Soviet planners are, however, eager for a generous infusion of Western technology if the price is right—which is to say, if available on cheap long-term credit or otherwise concessionary terms. The response called for is economic aid, which might seem to weld a stronger bond of dependency than a network of trade. But, historically, tribute has been no more successful than trade in preventing conquest or domination by a foreign power.

A Balance of Power

Perhaps the weakest link in Kissinger's argument is the insistence that any gains accruing to Soviet power from détente are irrelevant "because when both sides possess such enormous power, small additional increments cannot be translated into tangible advantage or even usable political strength.". . . . The power balance is still subject to infinite variation through "marginal adjustments."

Consider what has been happening to Soviet and American defense efforts in real terms. Ours has fallen by almost a sixth since 1964 while theirs (according to our official estimate) has risen by more than a third, coming to surpass ours by 1970. When the incremental cost of the Vietnam War is eliminated, our defense effort shows virtually a steady decline, year by year, since 1963. Theirs shows a steady rise. Are we to believe that this "marginal adjustment" has had no effect on the global power balance?

The most immediate impact has been on relative forces in being. In the strategic nuclear sphere, the Soviet Union has moved from a position of substantial inferiority to rough parity, a development that has made the balance of conventional forces, whose importance Kissinger has always stressed, all the more significant. The Soviet Union now has almost twice as many men under arms as we do; a decade ago it had only a sixth more than we did. Our surface combat fleet has shrunk in numbers to become smaller than the Soviet fleet; a decade ago it was a third larger. And so on and on. These divergent trends in military strength surely have implications for diplomacy as well as deterrence, as Kissinger, an avid practitioner of show of force, well knows. And, however unthinkable nuclear war has become, use of conventional force remains habitual: witness the instances of the last quarter century in Korea, Hungary, the Middle East, Africa, South Asia, Cuba, Southeast Asia, Czechoslovakia, and Cyprus.

Over the longer run, diverging defense efforts are likely to disturb the power balance more fundamentally, because the technology of weaponry, offensive and defensive, is in constant flux along with the military arts. There is no way to regulate this dynamic process through arms control without rigorous on-site inspection, and whichever power gains the upper hand in innovation achieves the potential for commanding the future heights of power. The nature of the military balance a decade hence is therefore being determined in the laboratories and on the proving grounds of today. Who knows what new miracles of horror science has in store for us? Perhaps they will metamorphose the balance of terror in the same way that nuclear explosives once did. Whether radical or not, change is certain in military art and science, and relative strength in research and development now is likely to be translated directly into future relative strength in being.

Examining the Alternatives

Much more could be said against détente, but it would repeat what can be found in a voluminous literature already in print. Enough has been said here to enable us to turn to the questions put by Secretary Kissinger to his critics:

> What is the alternative they propose? What precise policies do they want us to change? Are they prepared for a prolonged situation of dramatically increased international danger? Do they wish to return to the constant crises and high arms budgets of the cold war? Does détente encourage repression—or is it détente that has generated the ferment and the demands for openness that we are now witnessing? Can we ask our people to support confrontation unless they know that every reasonable alternative has been explored?

The questions are quite loaded, of course, because they imply that the critics must choose either white hat or black, either détente or cold war. If that is the only choice open, one wonders what has happened to the "new stable structure of peace" under construction these last six years. As Professor [Albert] Wohlstetter points out, "what is odd about this metaphor is its desire to have it both ways. The Structure of Peace in the nuclear era is solid and unshakable. Yet we must tiptoe carefully to make sure that we do not bring the whole apparently ramshackle affair crashing down about our ears in the final apocalypse of shattered glass and toppling masonry."

The metaphor is wrong on both counts: the structure is in fact shaky, but there is no need to tiptoe around our relations with the

Soviet Union. Not yet. An alternative stance is still achievable for American foreign policy that avoids the perils of Kissinger's détente at the one extreme and stark cold war at the other. It involves restoring Western confidence and resolve, reconstituting deterrence, basing negotiation firmly on the principles of reciprocal concession and unimpaired security, and bargaining accordingly.

As already stressed, Kissinger's diplomacy has created too much one-sided détente, an overrelaxation of tension in the United States and throughout the West. Tension is after all the natural defensive reaction to a perceived threat, and it alerts and stimulates the will to resist. Tension had become excessive in the West, Kissinger concluded, because the cold war associated with it contained a more perilous risk—nuclear annihilation—than the threat being resisted. Tension was relaxed by a diplomatic blitz that had the effect of accenting the nuclear risk while belittling the Soviet threat. The consequence has been a dangerous weakening of the will to resist, as a confused public tries to understand whether resistance is unnecessary or whether it is futile.

What needs to be done first is to restore a healthy state of alert based on appreciation of the external dangers threatening the Western way of life and a sense of confidence that they can be overcome. This can be done gradually by nudging diplomacy away from a quest for ways of getting the Soviet Union involved and toward the practice of quid-pro-quo bargaining. The differing nature of Eastern and Western problems provides a basis for reciprocal concessions benefitting both sides while improving Western security, or at least leaving it unimpaired.

Withholding Assistance

The Soviet Union suffers chronically from a defective economy, which constantly thwarts the ambition of Soviet leaders to maximize power in the future as well as now. The economy simply cannot meet the heavy demands placed on it for both maintaining strength in being and providing growth, including a rising living standard. The problems stem from the inefficient organization and deficient incentives of a huge command economy hampered by, among other things, a policy of basic autarky. Hence the economy experiences periodic agricultural crises in the short run and inability to generate a broad front of technological innovation over the long run.

One way out would be fundamental reform of the economic system, but the totalitarian rulers have carefully avoided such a venture for fear of undermining their monolithic power. Curing the patient might eliminate need for the doctor. And so they have turned predictably to the West for help.

Whatever economic help we give is bound to enhance Soviet power—to make it stronger than it otherwise would be. Gains to the West, if any, will be trivial economically and even more so strategically, because Western military and political strength is not constrained significantly by economic factors. Hence we should not help the Soviet Union economically and technologically unless we receive political concessions in return that leave our security at least unimpaired. In general we should insist on improvement of security since what the Soviet Union gains from economic aid and expanded trade strengthens the leadership internally as well as externally. It should be required to reduce the Soviet threat to the West in exchange for the gain in domestic power. It is on this basis that we should parley for Soviet movement on SALT [Strategic Arms Limitation Talks], MBFR [Mutual and Balanced Force Reduction], arms control in the Middle East, neutralization of Southeast Asia, and so on.

We must not delude ourselves that our foreign policy has no effect on conditions inside the Soviet Union and Eastern Europe. On this score, [Alexander] Solzhenitsyn is right and Kissinger wrong. If Soviet rulers know the West will bail them out of every economic difficulty, they will be under no pressure to liberalize the regime. Similarly, the relaxing of external tension has always been accompanied in the East by a tightening internally. Kissinger asks whether détente encourages repression or ferment, and the answer is repression. Dissent reached its high mark in the Soviet Union before détente, and the movement has been virtually stamped out since. The various parts of Eastern Europe have experienced a like reactionary policy. Kissinger attacks a straw man when he stubbornly insists that Western foreign policy cannot transform the Soviet domestic structure, for no one seriously believes that outside pressure can cause democracy or anything like it to spring forth overnight in Soviet society. That is not the issue at all, but rather how best to endorse and strengthen the liberal cause in the East.

Businesslike bargaining based on the principle of unimpaired security is hardly confrontation or cold war. If Soviet leaders blindly reject opportunities to make arrangements yielding mutual gains but not undermining our strategic position, we have all the less reason to believe that they will behave responsibly merely to continue enjoying the goodies of involvement.

Raising Confidence and Morale

A revitalized diplomacy will help raise Western morale and confidence and lay the way for repairing our crumbling ramparts and alliances. The downward trend of defense must be reversed or all else is in vain. NATO must be put back together again and its strategic dilemmas resolved. It is a sad fact that Western military strategy has lagged far behind technology, particularly in not appreciating the revolutionary significance of smart weapons, nonnuclear as well as nuclear. Selective strategic targeting, the product of intensive deliberation in the Pentagon in recent years, is an early sign of overdue revision of strategic doctrine.

The issue, then, is how to make best use of our assets in the continuing struggle to defend Western civilization against the threat from the East. Stripped of rhetoric, Kissinger's détente amounts to giving the assets away without requiring any strategic benefits in return, this being done on the premise that the Soviet rulers will so treasure what they are receiving that they will carefully avoid upsetting the strategic equilibrium. But, as we have argued, they will hardly need to do anything since the power balance will steadily move in their favor anyhow. The alternative proposed here would exchange our assets only for compensatory strategic benefits. Such a diplomacy of reciprocal concession holds far more promise for meaningful peace than the drift of détente.

Viewpoint 3

"I call upon the scientific community in our country . . . to give us the means of rendering . . . nuclear weapons impotent and obsolete."

The United States Must Develop a Defensive Weapons System to Prevent Nuclear War

Ronald Reagan

Ronald Reagan, who served as U.S. president from 1981 to 1989, rejected détente, the relaxation of tension between the United States and Soviet Union, and took a hard-line stand against America's adversary. During Reagan's first term, relations between the United States and the Soviet Union became strained, but during his second term, his growing friendship with Soviet leader Mikhail Gorbachev improved U.S.-Soviet relations. However, relations between the superpowers chilled once again in 1985, when Reagan proposed the Strategic Defense Initiative (SDI), the technological pursuit of defensive

Ronald Reagan, televised address, March 23, 1983.

weapons in space. Gorbachev's concern over SDI stalled negotiations on an intermediate-range nuclear forces (INF) treaty.
Both leaders ultimately signed the treaty in 1987.

In the following viewpoint, taken from an address to the nation televised on March 23, 1983, Reagan explains his reasons
for pursuing SDI, dubbed "Star Wars" after the popular science
fiction movie. According to Reagan, Soviet advances in "offensive" nuclear weapons technology had altered the balance of
power. Rather than build more offensive weapons in response,
which Reagan argued would accelerate the arms race and further jeopardize national security, the United States should develop a defensive system capable of destroying nuclear warheads
launched at the United States. The purpose of SDI would therefore be to restore balance between the two nations and prevent
nuclear war.

M y fellow Americans, thank you for sharing your time with
me tonight.

The subject I want to discuss with you, peace and national security, is both timely and important. Timely, because I've reached
a decision which offers a new hope for our children in the 21st
century, a decision I'll tell you about in a few minutes. And important because there's a very big decision that you must make for
yourselves. This subject involves the most basic duty that any President and any people share, the duty to protect and strengthen the
peace. . . .

A Strategy of Deterrence

The defense policy of the United States is based on a simple
premise: The United States does not start fights. We will never be
an aggressor. We maintain our strength in order to deter and defend against aggression—to preserve freedom and peace.

Since the dawn of the atomic age, we've sought to reduce the
risk of war by maintaining a strong deterrent and by seeking genuine arms control. "Deterrence" means simply this: making sure
any adversary who thinks about attacking the United States, or
our allies, or our vital interests, concludes that the risks to him

outweigh any potential gains. Once he understands that, he won't attack. We maintain the peace through our strength; weakness only invites aggression.

This strategy of deterrence has not changed. It still works. But what it takes to maintain deterrence has changed. It took one kind of military force to deter an attack when we had far more nuclear weapons than any other power; it takes another kind now that the Soviets, for example, have enough accurate and powerful nuclear weapons to destroy virtually all of our missiles on the ground. Now, this is not to say that the Soviet Union is planning to make war on us. Nor do I believe a war is inevitable—quite the contrary. But what must be recognized is that our security is based on being prepared to meet all threats. . . .

The Soviet Buildup

For 20 years the Soviet Union has been accumulating enormous military might. They didn't stop when their forces exceeded all requirements of a legitimate defensive capability. And they haven't stopped now. During the past decade and a half, the Soviets have built up a massive arsenal of new strategic nuclear weapons— weapons that can strike directly at the United States.

As an example, the United States introduced its last new intercontinental ballistic missile [ICBM], the Minute Man III, in 1969, and we're now dismantling our even older Titan missiles. But what has the Soviet Union done in these intervening years? Well, since 1969 the Soviet Union has built five new classes of ICBM's, and upgraded these eight times. As a result, their missiles are much more powerful and accurate than they were several years ago, and they continue to develop more, while ours are increasingly obsolete. . . .

But the Soviets are still adding an average of 3 new warheads a week, and now have 1,300. These warheads can reach their targets in a matter of a few minutes. We still have none. So far, it seems that the Soviet definition of parity is a box score of 1,300 to nothing, in their favor.

There was a time when we were able to offset superior Soviet numbers with higher quality, but today they are building weapons as sophisticated and modern as our own. . . .

An Offensive Military Force

Some people may still ask: Would the Soviets ever use their formidable military power? Well, again, can we afford to believe they won't? There is [the Soviet war in] Afghanistan. And in Poland, the Soviets denied the will of the people and in so doing demonstrated to the world how their military power could also be used to intimidate.

The final fact is that the Soviet Union is acquiring what can only be considered an offensive military force. They have continued to build far more intercontinental ballistic missiles than they could possibly need simply to deter an attack. Their conventional forces are trained and equipped not so much to defend against an attack as they are to permit sudden, surprise offensives of their own. . . .

Now, thus far tonight I've shared with you my thoughts on the problems of national security we must face together. My predecessors in the Oval Office [previous presidents] have appeared before you on other occasions to describe the threat posed by Soviet power and have proposed steps to address that threat. But since the advent of nuclear weapons, those steps have been increasingly directed toward deterrence of aggression through the promise of retaliation.

This approach to stability through offensive threat has worked. We and our allies have succeeded in preventing nuclear war for more than three decades. In recent months, however, my advisers, including in particular the Joint Chiefs of Staff, have underscored the necessity to break out of a future that relies solely on offensive retaliation for our security. . . .

A Defensive Strategy

Let me share with you a vision of the future which offers hope. It is that we embark on a program to counter the awesome Soviet missile threat with measures that are defensive. Let us turn to the very strengths in technology that spawned our great industrial base and that have given us the quality of life we enjoy today.

What if free people could live secure in the knowledge that their security did not rest upon the threat of instant U.S. retaliation to deter a Soviet attack, that we could intercept and destroy strategic ballistic missiles before they reached our own soil or that of our allies?

I know this is a formidable, technical task, one that may not be accomplished before the end of this century. Yet, current technology has attained a level of sophistication where it's reasonable for us to begin this effort. It will take years, probably decades of effort on many fronts. There will be failures and setbacks, just as there will be successes and breakthroughs. And as we proceed, we must remain constant in preserving the nuclear deterrent and maintaining a solid capability for flexible response. But isn't it worth every investment necessary to free the world from the threat of nuclear war? We know it is. . . .

Paving the Way for Peace

I clearly recognize that defensive systems have limitations and raise certain problems and ambiguities. If paired with offensive systems, they can be viewed as fostering an aggressive policy, and no one wants that. But with these considerations firmly in mind, I call upon the scientific community in our country, those who gave us nuclear weapons, to turn their great talents now to the cause of mankind and world peace, to give us the means of rendering these nuclear weapons impotent and obsolete.

Tonight, consistent with our obligations of the ABM [antiballistic missile] treaty and recognizing the need for closer consultation with our allies, I'm taking an important first step. I am directing a comprehensive and intensive effort to define a long-term research and development program to begin to achieve our ultimate goal of eliminating the threat posed by strategic nuclear missiles. This could pave the way for arms control measures to eliminate the weapons themselves. We seek neither military superiority nor political advantage. Our only purpose—one all people share—is to search for ways to reduce the danger of nuclear war.

My fellow Americans, tonight we're launching an effort which holds the promise of changing the course of human history. There will be risks, and results take time. But I believe we can do it. As we cross this threshold, I ask for your prayers and your support.

Viewpoint 4

"The purpose of [the Strategic Defense Initiative] is to achieve military superiority over the Soviet Union."

U.S. Development of a Defensive Weapons System Would Increase Nuclear Proliferation

Dmitri Klimov

Ronald Reagan, U.S. president from 1981 to 1989, was one of America's most popular presidents, yet his hard-line policy toward the Soviet Union encountered sharp criticism. Reagan's multibillion-dollar Strategic Defense Initiative (SDI), the technological pursuit of defensive weapons in space that critics dubbed "Star Wars" (after the popular science fiction movie), received particularly virulent criticism. Some argued that the system was wasteful and ineffective; others claimed that it would violate the 1972 U.S.-Soviet Antiballistic Missile (ABM) Treaty, which limited defensive systems.

Dmitri Klimov, "Five Years of SDI: What Next?" *Krasnaya Zvezda*, March 23, 1988.

In the following viewpoint, taken from a March 23, 1988, article published in the Soviet military newspaper *Krasnaya Zvezda* (*Red Star*), Soviet author Dmitri Klimov explains why he thinks the SDI program is dangerous. According to Klimov, the true motive behind SDI is U.S. military superiority over the Soviet Union. Klimov also argues that the development of a defensive weapons system would prompt other nations, including the Soviet Union, to build counterweapons capable of eluding the system, thereby increasing nuclear proliferation.

It is five years since the day U.S. President Ronald Reagan proclaimed the program for the establishment of a large-scale ABM [antiballistic missile] system with space-based elements, which subsequently received the official title "Strategic Defense Initiative [SDI]." In our view, however, those who described it as the "Star Wars" program[1] were far more accurate.

Defensive or Offensive?

The president did not provide a clear definition of what the system he proposed would be like. But he declared that it was designed to make nuclear arms "impotent and obsolete" and so would remove the threat of nuclear war. In fact, that is far from true. The purpose of SDI is to achieve military superiority over the Soviet Union. In a statement to the Senate Armed Services Committee, Caspar Weinberger, then U.S. defense secretary, cynically admitted that. Here are his exact words: "If we were able to acquire a system that was efficient, and if we knew that it could make their weapons (that is, the Soviet Union's weapons) impotent, we would return to the situation where we were the only country to possess nuclear weapons."

The extremely dangerous nature of such a program was obvious right from the start. The very next day after Ronald Reagan's statement, Congressman Tom Downey declared that the president's proposal to build an ABM system in outer space "is a most

1. Critics dubbed the multibillion-dollar SDI weapons system "Star Wars," after the popular science fiction movie.

horrific and absurd idea." "The president believes that lasers and beam weapons would be defensive by nature, but it is quite obvious that this is not so," another congressman, Jim Moody (D-WI), pointed out. "The introduction of more sophisticated weapons," he continued, "can lead only to the introduction of more powerful counterweapons." Another congressman, Les AuCoin (D-WI), said these words: "The president wants military superiority. But the Soviets will not stand still or allow us to achieve superiority. Instead, they will create new weapons which will in turn be capable of neutralizing space weapons."

Circumventing the ABM Treaty

As though summing up all of these statements, the *New York Times* wrote that "the president decided to develop research work on a new type of ABM system, despite the fact that many of his aides at the White House and the Defense Department believed that this idea had not been studied sufficiently." Valid concern was also aroused by the fact that the implementation of SDI runs counter to the 1972 Soviet-U.S. treaty on the limitation of ABM systems. It is no coincidence that even now, in the early stages of SDI implementation, the administration is trying to circumvent its provisions by resorting to the so-called "broad interpretation" and, essentially, rejecting a number of the treaty's provisions.

The opposition to the "Star Wars" program even among U.S. legislators is evidenced by the fact that Congress is systematically reducing the administration's requests for funds to be allocated to SDI. Thus, the requests for fiscal 1988 were cut from $5.7 billion to $3.9 billion. Nor has the idea of a "broad interpretation" of the ABM treaty met with the expected support in the Senate.

Nevertheless, the United States has been carrying out intensive development in the ABM sphere throughout these five years. Although Lieutenant General James Abrahamson, who heads the SDI organization, has acknowledged that budget cuts have somewhat slowed down the pace of research, he has, however, declared that the SDI organization has entirely abandoned the examination of only a small number of systems.

A considerable role is undoubtedly played here by pressure from the military-industrial corporations, which reckon on making superprofits out of implementing the program. But probably no less significant is the fact that the champions of "Star Wars" have managed to enlist considerable support by means of a forceful propaganda campaign. For the average American, who does not understand all the subtleties of foreign and military policy, the

A Battlefield in Space

In the following excerpt the Union of Concerned Scientists express their concerns about U.S. president Ronald Reagan's Strategic Defense Initiative (SDI), dubbed "Star Wars" after the popular science fiction movie. In theory SDI would be capable of destroying any nuclear warhead launched at the United States.

The vision of a perfect defense is immensely attractive, but it raises complex questions. Can Star Wars eliminate the threat of nuclear annihilation and end the arms race? Or is it an illusion that science can re-create the world that disappeared when the nuclear bomb was born? Will the attempt to install space defenses instead precipitate a nuclear conflict that could not be confined to space? These questions have intertwined political and technical strands. They must be examined carefully before the United States commits itself to the quest for a missile defense, because such a commitment would carry the nation—and the world— across a great divide.

If the president's vision is pursued, outer space could become a battlefield. An effective defense against a missile attack must employ weapons operating in space. This now peaceful sanctuary, so long a symbol of cooperation, would be violated. And the arduous process of arms control, which has scored so few genuine successes in the nuclear era, would also be imperiled—perhaps terminated—by the deployment of weapons in space.

John Tirman, *The Fallacy of Star Wars*, 1984.

promises to safeguard the country against a possible nuclear strike with the help of a "space shield" appear very alluring. Many Americans have been enthralled by the usual illusions and stereotypes. So many people in the United States, even those who are skeptical about SDI, deem it necessary to continue research to find out whether it is possible, from a scientific and technical viewpoint, to create a strategic defense system.

Questioning "Star Wars" Technology

What is the position today of this widely publicized program? The signing of the Soviet-U.S. treaty on intermediate- and shorter-range missiles (the INF treaty), which has opened up new prospects for the achievement of corresponding agreements, above all for a 50 percent reduction in strategic offensive arms, has still further increased skepticism about it. "SDI makes a nuclear war more likely," Eugene Carroll, deputy director of Washington's Center for Defense Information, emphasized, "because it pushes toward a buildup of offensive nuclear arms. And yet it is precisely this process that the United States and the Soviet Union are seeking to reverse during the Geneva talks on reducing strategic arms." This is why such fundamental significance is attached to a clause of the Soviet-U.S. joint statement signed in Washington on December 10, 1987, that the two countries' leaders have entrusted their delegations in Geneva with "elaborating an accord obliging the sides to observe the ABM Treaty in the form in which it was signed in 1972 in the process of carrying out the research, development, and, where necessary, testing permitted under the ABM Treaty and not to abrogate the ABM Treaty during the agreed term."

The U.S. press reports that SDI has also encountered a number of purely technical problems. In the opinion of U.S. specialists, its command and management programs, without which the whole system cannot function, are "suffering total failure." *Newsweek* magazine, for example, believes that "unless there is some unforeseen technological leap, SDI is threatened with gradually fading away." However, champions of "Star Wars" are seeking to give it a new boost and to achieve its unconditional implementation. Attempts are being made to technically revamp the program. Tests within the SDI framework are designed, in the opinion of its adherents, to convince skeptics of the program's efficiency and technical feasibility.

Thus, in December 1987, the first ground tests of a laser codenamed "Zenith Star" were conducted on a California range. And in February 1988 another SDI-related experiment was conducted, "Delta-181," during which a laser radar device was put into orbit and tested. Originally this experiment, which cost $250 million, was declared "very successful." However, it later became known that one of the sensors, the most important among the other analogous instruments launched into space, had gone out of commission.

Certain U.S. figures are already proposing the rejection of the ambitious plans to create a "space shield" and the reorientation of research within the SDI framework toward developing a considerably more modest system. But this is a complex issue. Thus, Senator Sam Nunn has proposed turning SDI into a "sensible defense initiative." "If we cautiously changed the thrust of our research, it could enable us to develop a limited system to counter the frightening possibility of an accidental or unsanctioned launch," Nunn declared. But champions of SDI are inclined to regard this proposal as a first step toward deploying a large-scale ABM system with space-based elements. This was said by Abrahamson, in particular, who called Nunn's proposal "very constructive."

Viewpoint 5

"It is . . . for fighting and winning the Cold War that Ronald Reagan deserves the most credit."

Ronald Reagan's Policies Ended the Cold War

Margaret Thatcher

Margaret Thatcher, Great Britain's first female prime minister, served during Ronald Reagan's tenure as U.S. president (1981–1989) and joined him in opposition to the Soviet Union. In the following viewpoint, taken from a speech to the Heritage Foundation's "Leadership for America" gala on December 12, 1998, Thatcher argues that it was the Reagan Doctrine that won the Cold War. According to Thatcher, appeasement of the Soviet Union weakened the West. When Reagan took office, Thatcher maintains, he took an aggressive stand against communism and convinced the American people that U.S. military superiority was necessary to oppose Soviet domination. Reagan's stance against communism was vindicated, she contends, when the Soviet Union released control of its Eastern European satellites, signaling the end of the Cold War.

President [Ronald] Reagan is one of the greatest men of our time and one of the greatest American presidents of all time. If that is not fully appreciated today, and sadly it is not, it isn't really surprising. After all, so many people have been proved wrong by Reagan that they simply daren't acknowledge his achievement. Forests already have been pulped to print the revisionist analyses of the eighties. Those who once were so confident of the superiority of the Soviet system that they advocated appeasement of it now pretend to believe that it was doomed to inevitable collapse. Tell that to the Russians! The former Soviet ministers didn't—and don't—doubt the seriousness of the struggle, even if Western liberal commentators do.

Reagan's Vision

Today we are particularly conscious of the courage of Ronald Reagan. He set out to challenge everything the liberal political elite of America accepted and sought to propagate. They believed that America was doomed to decline. He believed it was destined for further greatness. They imagined that sooner or later there would be a convergence between the free Western system and the socialist Eastern system, and that some kind of social democratic outcome was inevitable. He, by contrast, considered that socialism was a patent failure which should be cast onto the trash heap of history.

It is, however, for fighting and winning the Cold War that Ronald Reagan deserves the most credit—and credit not just from Americans but from the rest of what we called in those days the Free World and from those in the former communist states who now can breathe the air of liberty.

Of course, there always were some honest men struggling to arrest the decline, or at least to ameliorate its consequences. The doctrine of "containment" was envisaged as a way of conducting a strategic resistance to communist incursion. Similarly, the doctrine of "détente" also had its honorable Western advocates, but the fact remains that it meant different things to different sides.

Heading Toward Defeat

For the West, détente signified—as the word itself literally means— an easing in tension between two superpowers and two blocs. This made a certain sense at the time because it reduced the risk of a nuclear confrontation, which Western unpreparedness had brought closer because we had allowed our conventional defenses to run down. But it also threatened to lead us into a fatal trap for, to the Soviets, détente signified merely the promotion of their goal of world domination while minimizing the risk of direct military confrontation. So under the cloak of wordy communiqués about peace and understanding the Soviet Union expanded its nuclear arsenal and its navy, engaged in continual doctrinal warfare and subverted states around the globe by means of its own advisers and the armed forces of its surrogates. There was only one destination to which this path could lead—that of Western defeat. And that's where we were heading.

The Soviet Union was dangerous—deadly dangerous—but the danger was that from a wounded predator, not some proud beast of the jungle.

The more intelligent Soviet apparatchiks had grasped that the economic and social system of the USSR was crumbling. . . . It would have to rely for its survival on the ability to terrify its opponents with the same success as it had terrified its own citizens.

A totally planned society and economy has the ability to concentrate productive capacity on some fixed objective with a reasonable degree of success and do it better than liberal democracies. But totalitarianism can only work like this for a relatively short time, after which the waste, distortions and corruption increase intolerably. So the Soviet Union had to aim at global dominance and achieve it quickly because, given a free competition between systems, no one would wish to choose that of the Soviets. Their problem was that even though they diverted the best of their talent and a huge share of their gross domestic product to the military complex, they lacked the moral and material resources to achieve superiority. That would be apparent as soon as the West found leaders determined to face them down.

The Reagan Doctrine

This was what Reagan, with my enthusiastic support and that of a number of other leaders, set out to do as president. And he did it on the basis of a well-considered and elaborate doctrine.

The world has, of course, seen many international doctrines—
[James] Monroe, [Harry S.] Truman and [Leonid] Brezhnev all
have made their contributions, some more posture than others.
But for my money it is the Reagan Doctrine . . . that has had the
best and the greatest impact. This was a rejection of both containment and détente . . . the struggle with communism was over.
The West henceforth would regard no area of the world as destined to forego its liberty simply because the Soviets claimed it to
be within their sphere of influence. We would fight a battle of
ideas against communism and we would give material support to
those who fought to recover their nations from tyranny.

Reagan could have no illusion about the opposition he would
face at home on this course: He had, after all, seen these forces
weaken the West throughout the seventies. But he used his inim-
itable ability to speak to the hearts of the American people and to
appeal over the heads of the cynical, can't-do elite. He and [former
defense secretary] Cap Weinberger made no secret of the objective: military superiority. The Soviets understood more quickly
than his domestic critics the seriousness of what was at stake. The
Russian rhetoric became more violent, but an understanding that
the game was up gradually dawned in the recesses of the Politburo.

The Soviet power brokers knew they had to choose a reformer
because they understood that the old strategy of intimidating and
subverting would not work with Reagan in the White House
and—who knows?—even Margaret Thatcher in 10 Downing
Street [in London].

The Strategic Defense Initiative

The final straw for the Evil Empire was the Strategic Defense Initiative, or SDI. Reagan was, I believe, deliberately and cunningly
tempted by the Soviets at [the superpower summit in] Reykjavik
[Iceland]. They made ever more alluring offers to cut their nuclear
arsenals and the president, who was a genuine believer in a nuclear-
weapons-free world (it was one of the few things we disagreed
about), thought he was making progress. There was no mention
of SDI, and it appeared that the Soviets tacitly had accepted that its
future was not for negotiation. Then, at the very last moment they
insisted that SDI effectively be abandoned. The president imme-

diately refused, the talks ended in acrimony and in the media he was heavily criticized. But it was on that day, when a lesser man would have compromised, that he showed his mettle.

As a result of his courage, work on the SDI program continued and the Soviets understood that their last gambit had failed. Three years later, when Mikhail Gorbachev peacefully allowed Eastern Europe to slide out of Soviet control, Reagan's earlier decision to stand firm was vindicated. The Soviets at last understood that the best they could hope for was to be allowed to reform their system, not to impose it on the rest of the world. And, of course, as soon as they embarked upon serious reform the artificial construct of the USSR, sustained by lies and violence for more than half a century, imploded with a whimper.

A Quiet Courage

The idea that such achievements were a matter of luck frankly is laughable. Yes, the president had luck. But he deserved the luck he enjoyed. Fortune favors the brave, the saying runs. As this hero of our times faces his final and most merciless enemy, he shows the same quiet courage which allowed him to break the world free of a monstrous creed without a shot being fired.

Political courage constantly will be required to restate the case for Western unity under American leadership. America was left by the end of the Cold War as the effective global power of last resort, the only superpower. But there also was a widespread reluctance to face up to this reality. The same mentality which Reagan had had to overcome was at work. Large numbers of intellectuals and commentators, uneasy at the consequences of victory whose causes they had never properly understood, sought to submerge America and the West in a new, muddled multilateralism. I suppose it is not surprising. As [Professor] Irving Kristol once noted, "No modern nation has ever constructed a foreign policy that was acceptable to its intellectuals."

Today's international policymakers have succumbed to a liberal contagion whose most alarming symptom is to view any new and artificial structure as preferable to a traditional and tested one. So they forget that it was powerful nation-states, drawing on national loyalties and national armies, that enforced U.N. Security Council resolutions and defeated Iraq in 1991. Their short-term goal is to subordinate American and other national sovereignties to multilateral authorities; their long-term goal, one suspects, is to establish the United Nations as a kind of embryo world government.

A Duty to Lead

International relations today are in a kind of limbo. Few politicians and diplomats really believe that any power other than the United States can guarantee the peace or punish aggression. But neither is there sufficient cohesion in the West to give America the moral and material support she must have to fulfill that role.

This has to change. America's duty is to lead. The other Western countries' duty is to support its leadership. Provided Western countries unite under American leadership, the West will remain the dominant global influence; if we do not, the opportunity for rogue states and new tyrannical powers to exploit our divisions will increase, and so will the danger to all.

These are as much tasks of today as they were of yesterday, as much the duty of conservative believers now as they were when Reagan and I refused to accept the decline of the West as our ineluctable destiny. As the poet said: "That which the fathers bequeathed thee, earn it anew if thou would'st possess it."

Viewpoint 6

"Gorbachev both understood and successfully charted the course that led to the end of the Cold War."

Mikhail Gorbachev's Policies Ended the Cold War

Raymond L. Garthoff

Because the Cold War was based upon the Soviet worldview that conflict between communism and capitalism was inevitable, only a Soviet leader could end the Cold War, argues Raymond L. Garthoff in the following viewpoint. Mikhail Gorbachev, who rejected this worldview, led the Soviet Union away from confrontation and toward cooperation, thus transforming Soviet policy and ending the Cold War. According to Garthoff, Gorbachev believed that maintaining a balance of interests rather than a balance of power should be the basis of the Soviet Union's relationship with the rest of the world. As a result, Garthoff maintains, Gorbachev negotiated arms reduction agreements, increased Soviet support for United Nations peacekeeping efforts, and convinced the Soviet Communist Party to accept the transition of Eastern European nations from Soviet-allied states into non-Communist neutral states and, ultimately, German unification. Garthoff is a senior fellow in the Brookings

Raymond L. Garthoff, "Looking Back: The Cold War in Retrospect," *Brookings Review*, Summer 1994. Copyright © 1994 by the Brookings Institution. Reproduced by permission.

Institution for Foreign Policy Studies program and author of *The Great Transition: American-Soviet Relations and the End of the Cold War*, from which this viewpoint is adapted.

The Soviet Union and the United States waged the Cold War in the belief that confrontation was unavoidable, that it was imposed by history. Soviet leaders were convinced that communism would ultimately triumph in the world and that the Soviet Union was the vanguard socialist-communist state. They were also convinced that the Western "imperialist" powers were historically bound to pursue a hostile course against them. For their part, American and other Western leaders assumed that the Soviet Union was determined to enhance its power and to pursue expansionist policies by all expedient means to achieve a Soviet-led communist world. Each side thought that it was compelled by the very existence of the other to engage in zero-sum competition, and each saw the unfolding history of the Cold War as confirming its views.

The prevailing Western view was wrong in attributing a master plan to the Kremlin,[1] in believing that communist ideology impelled Soviet leaders to expand their power, in exaggerating communist abilities to subvert a Free World, and in thinking that Soviet officials viewed military power as an ultimate recourse. But the West was not wrong in believing that Soviet leaders were committed to a historically driven struggle between two worlds until, in the end, theirs would triumph. To be sure, other motivations and interests, including national aims, institutional interests, and even personal psychological considerations, played a part. These influences, however, tended to enhance the ideological framework rather than weaken it. Moreover, the actions of each side were sufficiently consistent with the ideological expectations of the other side to sustain their respective worldviews for many years.

Within that ideological framework, the Americans and the Soviets carried on the Cold War as a geopolitical struggle, based more realistically on traditional balance-of-power politics than on

1. the government of Russia and formerly that of the Soviet Union

world class struggle or global containment and deterrence theory. If ideology alone had driven the superpowers, the Cold War would be seen as arising from the October Revolution of 1917[2] rather than from the ashes of World War II. But in 1917 and during the next 25 years the Soviet Union was relatively weak and only one of several great powers in a multipolar world. By the end of World War II, however, Germany and Japan had been crushed, Britain, France, and China were weakened, and the Soviet Union, even though much weaker than the United States, seemed to pose an unprecedented threat by virtue of its massive armies and their presence deep in Central Europe. Under these circumstances, [Soviet leader] Josef Stalin's reassertion in 1946 and 1947 of the division of the world into two contending camps seemed more valid and more threatening than ever before.

Thus charged by geopolitical circumstances, a Manichean communist worldview spawned a Manichean[3] anticommunist worldview. Each side imputed unlimited objectives, ultimately world domination, to the other. Each side looked to realize its ambitions (or its historical destiny) over the long term and thus posited an indefinite period of conflict. But even though both sides envisioned a conflict of indefinite duration, and even though policy decisions were pragmatic and based on calculation of risk, cost, and gain, the hazard of a miscalculation always existed. And that could be fatally dangerous, given the historical coincidence of the Cold War and the first half-century of the nuclear age. Nuclear weapons, by threatening the existence of world civilization, added significantly to the tension of the epoch; the stakes were utterly without precedent and beyond full comprehension.

Setting Change in Motion

Nuclear weapons also helped to keep the Cold War cold, to prevent a third world war in the 20th century. Nonetheless, in the fi-

2. An uprising that was part of a violent upheaval in Russia in 1917. The uprising resulted in the overthrow of the czarist government, ultimately replacing it with a Communist government.   3. *Manichean* refers to a belief in the doctrines of Manes, a Persian of the third century A.D., who taught a dualism in which light is regarded as the source of good and darkness as the source of evil. Here, both the Communists and anti-Communists see themselves as good and the other as evil.

nal analysis and despite their awesome power, nuclear weapons did not cause, prevent, or end the Cold War, which would have been waged even had such weapons never existed. The arms race and other aspects of the superpower rivalry were, however, driven in part by ideological assumptions. As a result, while the Cold War and the nuclear arms race could be attenuated when opportunities or constraints led both sides to favor relaxing tensions, neither could be ended until the ideological underpinnings of the confrontation had fallen. And fall they did—under the leadership of [Soviet leader] Mikhail Gorbachev, who set in motion a fundamental reevaluation of the processes at work in the real world, a basic reassessment of threats, and finally a deep revision of Moscow's aims and political objectives. The United States and the West in general were cautious but eventually recognized this fundamental change and reciprocated.

The West did not, as is widely believed, win the Cold War through geopolitical containment and military deterrence. Still less was the Cold War won by the Reagan military buildup and the Reagan Doctrine,[4] as some have suggested. Instead, "victory" came when a new generation of Soviet leaders realized how badly their system at home and their policies abroad had failed. What containment did do was to preclude any temptations on the part of Moscow to advance Soviet hegemony by military means. It is doubtful that any postwar Soviet leadership would have deliberately resorted to war. That was not, however, so clear to many at the time. Deterrence may have been redundant, but at the least it was highly successful in providing reassurance to the peoples of Western Europe. For four decades it performed the historic function of holding Soviet power in check, or being prepared to do so, until the internal seeds of destruction in the Soviet Union and its empire could mature. At that point, however, Gorbachev transformed Soviet policy and brought the Cold War to an end.

Despite important differences among them, all Soviet leaders before Gorbachev had shared a belief in an ineluctable conflict be-

---

4. Ronald Reagan assumed that the Soviet Union could not be trusted and therefore undertook a policy of supplying military aid to rebellious peoples who hoped to free themselves of Soviet domination.

tween socialism and capitalism. Although Gorbachev remained a socialist, and in his own terms even a communist, he renounced the Marxist-Leninist-Stalinist idea of inevitable world conflict. His avowed acceptance of the interdependence of the world, of the priority of human values over class values, and of the indivisibility of common security marked a revolutionary ideological change. That change, which Gorbachev publicly declared as early as February 1986 (though it was then insufficiently noted), manifested itself in many ways during the next five years, in deeds as well as words, including policies reflecting a drastically reduced Soviet perception of the Western threat and actions to reduce the Western perception of a Soviet threat.

In 1986, for example, Gorbachev made clear his readiness to ban all nuclear weapons. In 1987 he signed the Intermediate-range Nuclear Forces Treaty, eliminating not only the Soviet and U.S. missiles deployed since the late 1970s but also the whole of the Soviet strategic theater missile forces that had faced Europe and Asia for

---

"It's Alive!"

In this cartoon, Soviet leader Mikhail Gorbachev, who can be identified by the birthmark on his forehead, is portrayed as a mad scientist who, in the eyes of Communists, experimented with the Soviet government and created a monster—democracy.

Cullum. © 1991 by Copley News Service. Reprinted with permission.

---

three decades. What is more, the treaty instituted an intrusive and extensive verification system. In 1988 Gorbachev proposed conventional arms reductions in Europe under a plan that would abandon the Soviet Union's numerical superiority, and he launched a substantial unilateral force reduction. In 1988–89 he withdrew all Soviet forces from Afghanistan. At about the same time, he encouraged the ouster of the old communist leadership in Eastern Europe and accepted the transition of the former Soviet-allied states into noncommunist neutral states. By 1990 he had signed the Conventional Forces in Europe Treaty accepting Soviet conventional arms levels much lower than NATO's [North Atlantic Treaty Organization]. By that time he had not only accepted Germany's reunification but also the membership of a united Germany in NATO. Within another year he had jettisoned the Warsaw Pact and the socialist bloc and agreed, in the Strategic Arms Reduction Treaty, to verified deep cuts in strategic nuclear forces.

A New Concept of Security

Although Gorbachev had not expected the complete collapse of communism (and Soviet influence) in Eastern Europe that took place in 1989 and 1990, he had made clear to the 27th Congress of the Soviet Communist Party as early as February 1986 that a new conception of security had to replace the previous one, and that the confrontation of the Cold War had to end. No longer speaking in Leninist terms of contending socialist and capitalist worlds, Gorbachev spoke instead of one world, an "interdependent and in many ways integral world." He denied that any country could find security in military power, either for defense or deterrence. Security, he said, could be found only through political means and only on a mutual basis. The goal, he asserted, should be the "creation of a comprehensive system of international security" that embraced economic, ecological, and humanitarian, as well as political and military, elements. Hence, the Soviet decision to give new support to the United Nations (UN), including collective peacekeeping, and to join the world economic system. Hence, the cooperative Soviet efforts to resolve regional conflicts in Central America, Southern Africa, the Horn of Africa, Cambodia, Afghanistan, and the Middle East, not to mention the Soviet Union's support for the collective UN-endorsed action against Iraq in 1991. And hence Moscow's willingness to countenance the dissolution of the Eastern European alliance and socialist commonwealth, which had been fashioned to meet security requirements and ideological imperatives that had now been abandoned.

In the final analysis, because the Cold War rested on Marxist-Leninist assumptions of inevitable world conflict, only a Soviet leader could have ended it. And Gorbachev set out deliberately to do just that. Although earlier Soviet leaders had understood the impermissibility of war in the nuclear age, Gorbachev was the first to recognize that reciprocal political accommodation, rather than military power for deterrence or "counterdeterrence," was the defining core of the Soviet Union's relationship with the rest of the world. He accepted the idea of building relations on the basis of a "balance of interests" among nations, rather than trying to maximize the power of one state or bloc on the basis of a "correlation of forces," a balance of power. The conclusions that Gorbachev drew from this recognition, and consequent Soviet actions, finally permitted the Iron Curtain to be dismantled and the global confrontation of the Cold War to end.

Exaggerated Expectations

Gorbachev, to be sure, seriously underestimated the task of changing the Soviet Union, and his miscalculation led to policy errors that contributed to the failure of his program for transforming Soviet society and polity. His vision of a resurrected socialism built on the foundation of successful perestroika and demokratizatsiya[5] was never a realistic possibility. He knew deep economic reform was necessary, and he tried; he did not find the solution. A revitalized Soviet political union was perhaps beyond realization as well. The reasons for Gorbachev's failure were primarily objective, not subjective; that is, they were real obstacles he was unable to overcome—internal opposition, powerful inertia, intractable problems of economic transformation, and the politically charged

5. Perestroika involved the restructuring of the Soviet economy and bureaucracy that began in the mid-1980s. Demokratizatsiya is the process of post-Soviet democratization.

problem of redefining a democratic relationship between a traditional imperial center and the rest of the country—not unwillingness or inability to give up or modify his ideological presuppositions and predispositions.

In the external political arena, however, Gorbachev both understood and successfully charted the course that led to the end of the Cold War, even though in this area, too, at first he had an exaggerated expectation of the capacity for reform on the part of the communist governments in Eastern Europe.

America's Role

The American role in ending the Cold War was necessary but, naturally, not primary. How could it be when the American worldview was derivative of the communist worldview? Containment was hollow without an expansionist power to contain. In this sense, it was the Soviet threat, partly real and partly imagined, that generated the American dedication to waging the Cold War, regardless of what revisionist American historians have to say. These historians point to Washington's atomic diplomacy and to its various overt and covert political, economic, paramilitary, and military campaigns. Supposedly designed to counter a Soviet threat, they argue, these initiatives actually entailed an expansion of American influence and dominion.

The revisionist interpretation errs in attributing imperial initiative and design to American diplomacy, but it is not entirely wrong. American policymakers were guilty of accepting far too much of the communist worldview in constructing an anticommunist antipode, and of being too ready to fight fire with fire. . . .

True, the Cold War led in some instances to constructive American involvements. The Marshall Plan[6] is a prime example, not to mention American support for some democratic political movements and for the Congress for Cultural Freedom and the liberal journal *Encounter*. But overt and covert involvements were more frequently less constructive, and often subversive, of real liberalism and democracy. Apart from the loss of American lives and

---

6. Also known as the European Recovery Program of 1948, the Marshall Plan provided $13.3 billion in economic aid to a war-devastated Europe.

treasure in such misplaced ventures as the Vietnam War and in the massive overinvestment in weaponry, one of the worst effects of forcing all world developments onto the procrustean bed of the Cold War was the distortion of America's understanding and values. By dividing the globe into a communist Evil Empire controlled by Moscow and a Free World led by Washington, American policymakers promoted numerous antidemocratic regimes into membership in the Free World as long as they were anticommunist (or even rhetorically so). Washington also used the exigencies of the Cold War to justify assassination plots, to negotiate deals with war lords, drug lords, and terrorists, and to transform anticommunist insurgents, however corrupt or antidemocratic, into "freedom fighters." Alliance ties, military basing rights, and support for insurgencies were routinely given priority over such other American objectives as promoting nuclear nonproliferation, economic development, human rights, and democracy.

Parallel Soviet sins were at least as great. While Soviet foreign assistance to socialist and "progressive" countries was sometimes constructive (building the Aswan Dam, for example, or providing economic assistance to India), it was also skewed by the ideological expectation of moving the world toward communism and by expectations of Soviet geopolitical advantage in the Cold War. Often dictatorial regimes, "Marxist" or "socialist" only according to the cynical claims of their leaders, provided the basis for Soviet support, as with [Mohammad] Siad Barre in Somalia, for example, or Mengistu [Haile Mariam] in Ethiopia. The Soviet Union also engaged in many covert political operations and lent support to national liberation movements (some authentic, others less so) that sometimes included elements engaged in terrorism. On both sides, then, ideological beliefs combined with geopolitical considerations to fuel a Cold War struggle that left many victims in its wake.

A Reality Check

Although the decisive factor in the end of the Cold War was a change in these beliefs, it is worth repeating that the Soviet leaders could discard a long-encrusted and familiar ideology only because of a powerful transformation in the way Gorbachev and some colleagues perceived reality, and because they were ready to adapt domestic and foreign policies to the new perception. Over time, the extent and depth of these changes became inescapable and their validity compelling, bringing the Cold War to an end. The critical culminating event was the Revolution of '89.

The year between the destruction of the Berlin Wall in November 1989 and the European conference in Paris in November 1990 saw the removal of the most important manifestation of the Cold War: the division of Germany and Europe. The division of Europe had symbolized the global battle between the two ideological and geopolitical camps in the years immediately after World War II. When that division came to an end, the consequences for the international balance of power were so substantial that even the most hardened cold warriors in the West were forced to acknowledge that the Cold War had ended—even before the collapse of communist rule in the Soviet Union or of the Soviet Union itself. Moreover, the Revolution of '89 in Eastern Europe was decisive not only in demonstrating that the ideological underpinnings of the Cold War had been removed but also in shifting the actual balance of power. The removal of Soviet military power from Eastern Europe dissolved the threat to Western Europe and also restored a reunified Europe to the center of the world political stage. Russia and even the United States have now become less central. American-Russian relations nonetheless remain of great importance in the post–Cold War world.

CHAPTER 4

Reflections: The Impact of the Cold War

Chapter Preface

Many scholars argue that by seeing the Cold War as the triumph of democracy over communism, historians are blinded to post–Cold War social and environmental problems and the need for further development of democratic principles to include some elements of socialism. Cold War historian Paul Dukes maintains, "Because of the sense of triumph in the USA following the collapse of its longterm rival, these problems have not so far commanded the serious consideration they deserve."

The principles that guided the sociopolitical development of the United States and the Soviet Union evolved from European thought. The individualism advanced by the United States was a refinement of the concept of individual rights found in the Magna Carta of 1215, a document that articulated laws protecting the rights of English subjects that the king was compelled to observe. Eighteenth-century Russian empress Catherine the Great modeled Russian sociopolitical philosophy after the medieval principle that the responsibility of nobility was to protect the collective—the people of the village. She called this new, more beneficent form of absolute monarchy "enlightened absolutism." Scholars did not see these emerging sociopolitical philosophies as necessarily incompatible. In fact, in 1864 Alexander Herzen, a prominent nineteenth-century Russian social thinker, hoped that these two diverging political and economic concepts—American individuality and Russian collectivism—could converge into a higher form of existence: "The North American States and Russia represent two solutions which are opposite but incomplete, and therefore complement rather than exclude each other."

The Cold War is evidence that these two philosophies did not in fact converge, and neither alone proved to be a panacea. While democracy, with its emphasis on individual rights, gives each citizen a voice in government, capitalism, the economic system applied in the United States, stresses competition and profit. Many scholars grant that competition promotes innovation and stimulates economic growth, but argue that some businesses focus solely on increasing profits while exploiting workers, harming the environment, and ignoring the safety of consumers. Moreover, despite democracy's promises to ensure life, liberty, and the pursuit of happiness, many Americans, especially those from minority groups, live in poverty, which in turn limits their access to education and other opportunities. "In spite of the USA's apparent victory in the Cold War," Dukes contends, "these problems have not disappeared." According to like-minded scholars, the pursuit of individual freedom at the expense of others in the community prevents universal access to the rights envisioned by democratic ideals.

In contrast, the philosophy of socialism that had been developing in Russia since Catherine's time aimed to alleviate the inequities inherent in capitalism by placing property in the hands of the collective. By 1917, the Bolsheviks, a radical wing of the Social Democratic Party in Russia, had developed their own form of socialism—communism. The Bolsheviks advocated immediate and violent revolution to bring about the downfall of capitalism and the establishment of an international socialist state. Contrary to the hopes of Bolshevist theorists, the centralized Soviet government that emerged after the Russian revolution ultimately developed into a giant totalitarian state that dominated every aspect of life and violated the ideals of equality and individual liberty that its founders had advocated. This Soviet state violated the human rights of Soviet citizens who opposed it, and the monolithic bureaucracy created by the centralized government impeded Soviet economic development, which kept many Soviet citizens in poverty.

Neither the United States nor the Soviet Union achieved the ideals envisioned by its founders. To see the failure of Communist socialism and the triumph of democratic capitalism as an unmitigated good, scholars contend, can blind people to the economic, environmental, and social problems capitalist democracies continue to face. While the United States may have defeated the Soviet Union in the Cold War, in the eyes of many, the United States has failed to win the war against inequality within its own borders. For all people to experience liberty, these analysts claim, the pursuit of individual freedom must be balanced with the needs of the community, a notion central to socialism.

As early as 1947, Pulitzer Prize–winning poet and dramatist

Archibald MacLeish saw the flaws in both capitalism and communism, arguing, "Both Capitalism and Communism are products of the thinking and practice of earlier times. . . . The problem for our generation is not to take sides in an old, stale and more or less irrelevant quarrel, but to find and find quickly the new and unrealized means of living in a world never before inhabited by mankind." Whether or not democratic nations will look beyond triumphalism and work toward a more universal application of democratic principles remains to be seen. The authors in the following chapter look back on the Cold War from several angles, examining whether that forty-three-year struggle had an overall positive or negative impact on the world.

Viewpoint 1

"War between the superpowers did not occur, and common sense suggests that the possession of overwhelming nuclear capability by both sides probably had something to do with it."

Nuclear Deterrence Was an Effective Cold War Strategy

John Garnett

The strategy of nuclear deterrence prevented nuclear war and kept major conflicts such as the Korean War from escalating, argues John Garnett in the following selection. According to Garnett, the mutual vulnerability created by nuclear weapons convinced the leaders of the United States and the Soviet Union that the enemy could only be deterred from nuclear assaults by the threat of retaliation. In consequence, he argues, both superpowers increased their nuclear arsenals to levels matching what they believed the other had, an arms buildup that established a delicate, but effective, balance between the two nations. Although not an ideal solution, Garnett claims, in the end mutual deterrence helped prevent the superpowers from going to war. Garnett, coauthor with L.W. Martin of *British Foreign Policy: Challenges and Choices for the 21st Century*, is a professor of international politics at the University of Wales, Aberystwyth.

John Garnett, "Face to Face with Armageddon," *History Today*, vol. 49, March 1999, p. 34. Copyright © 1999 by History Today Ltd. Reproduced by permission.

Two developments, one technical, the other political, have shaped East-West relations for most of the second half of the twentieth century. The first was the development of nuclear and thermonuclear weapons together with delivery systems with intercontinental ranges. The second was the onset and evolution of the Cold War, which, though fluctuating in intensity, provided the political context in which the new weapons of mass destruction had to be evaluated. These twin developments led to the strategy of nuclear deterrence which came to dominate the military policies of both superpowers from the mid-1960s, and reflected and exacerbated the Cold War.

The Evolution of Deterrence

Gradually, deterrence evolved into a highly sophisticated body of related ideas about the role of nuclear weapons. But in the late 1940s, when the Cold War was just beginning, the complicated 'theology' of deterrence did not exist, and strategists and policymakers were still struggling with the implications of the newly invented atomic bomb. Everyone felt that a new era in destructive warfare had arrived, but even those who thought about it were not sure what this meant. Among some fairly wild speculation about 'push button warfare', 'suitcase bombs' and the imminence of Armageddon, some basic military realities were emerging. It became clear that there was no defence against these new weapons, that population centres were particularly vulnerable and that a surprise attack could give an aggressor a decisive advantage. It was this gloomy analysis which focused minds on nuclear deterrence and the belief that since states could no longer protect themselves by traditional measures, then enemies could, henceforth, only be deterred from aggression by the threat of devastating retaliation. This view provided the basic rationale for the most expensive military strategy the world has ever seen. . . .

Both superpowers accepted that their mutual vulnerability might not be such a bad thing. When that happened 'mutual deterrence' became a policy objective as well as a de facto situation, and from the mid-1960s onwards an enormous amount of effort was directed towards perpetuating it. In particular, East-West arms control negotiations enshrined mutual deterrence by eschewing any arms reductions which might threaten it and discouraging any military policies or technological developments likely to undermine it. Despite the rhetoric of disarmament, the management of mutual vulnerability rather than arms reduction became the keystone of the arms control policies of both sides. The bargaining was tough, but SALT [Strategic Arms Limitation Talks] I and II and the START [Strategic Arms Reduction Treaty] process all reflected attempts by the superpowers to manage strategic nuclear developments in such a way as to stabilise mutual deterrence. Ballistic missile defences were outlawed; 'first strike' weapons were decommissioned; civil defence was discouraged. In this curious 'adverse partnership', the two superpowers manipulated the arms race in the interests of mutual deterrence.

Maintaining a Stable Balance

Despite its critical role, there was much confusion, particularly in the early years of the Cold War, about what constituted mutual deterrence. Some confused it with the possession of nuclear capability by both sides. Others believed it arose when both sides had roughly the same number of nuclear weapons. However, strategists were quick to point out that there is a big difference between a balance of terror in which each side has the capacity to obliterate the other, and one in which both sides have that capacity no matter who strikes first. In other words, it is not the 'balance' of an arms race that constitutes mutual deterrence; it is the stability of the balance. A stable balance only exists when neither side in striking first can destroy the other's ability to strike back. Merely equalling or matching the weapons systems of the enemy misconstrues the nature of the problem. To deter an attack means being able to strike back in spite of it. It means being able to strike second with 'assured destruction' capability.

But even this is not quite true. Deterrence does not mean that both sides must have efficient retaliatory systems; it only means that each side must think the other has. This is so because deterrence is primarily a psychological phenomenon. If both sides have invulnerable deterrent forces, but neither side believes that the other has, then the situation is one of extreme instability, because each side will believe it could launch a successful attack. And if neither side has deterrent capacity, but both sides believe that the other has it, then the situation is one of mutual deterrence even if all the objective requirements are missing. In other words, whether or not a situation of mutual deterrence exists depends on the state of mind or the mental image which one side has of the other, and it is not automatically connected with real-world objective military capabilities.

The best way of seeming to have efficient deterrent capacity is to actually have it. Hence, if both sides are pursuing a policy of preventing war by mutual deterrence, they must seek invulnerable retaliatory weapons, which by definition, are capable of striking back after an attack by the enemy. Unfortunately, the ability to strike back after being attacked is by no means an automatic result of an arms race.

By the late 1950s the difficulties were beginning to be appreciated. Both superpowers recognised that the first requirement of an effective deterrent was that it should survive or 'ride out' a surprise 'counterforce' targeted attack without being decimated—a task made difficult by the ever increasing numbers of accurate delivery systems, 'penetration aids', and multiple warheads which entered service during the next thirty years. Technological innovation forced both sides to spend a fortune on protecting their retaliatory forces via early warning radars, diverse delivery vehicles, 'hardened' missile sites and submarine launched systems. . . . However, fearful that a technological breakthrough might undermine particular weapons even on submarines, both superpowers spread the risk by maintaining a 'triad' of forces, bombers, land-based missiles and submarine-launched missiles. Even if one leg of the triad became vulnerable the others would suffice to deter. . . .

A Reason to Be Nervous

The era of 'mutual assured destruction' (MAD) had arrived. Not everyone, though, was reassured by the stalemate that now existed. Though both sides recognised mutual deterrence as a de facto situation, neither was entirely convinced that the other had abandoned ideas of nuclear superiority and 'first strike' capability. There was particular unease in the US. The Soviets never seemed enthusiastic about mutual deterrence and were always reluctant to abandon ideas of ultimate victory in war. Technological improvements in missile guidance and multiple warheads did nothing to diminish suspicions on both sides. . . . The fact that the arms race showed no signs of slowing was a permanent source of tension and proved that the stability of the nuclear balance could not be taken for granted.

Another reason for nervousness about relying too heavily on the strategy of deterrence was an appreciation by strategists on both sides of the Iron Curtain[1] that it might fail. In much the same way that murderers are not deterred by the threat of life imprisonment or capital punishment, so, it was argued, aggressive states might not be deterred by the threat of nuclear retaliation. The question of what to do if deterrence failed was one with which both superpowers wrestled. In the event of an aggression the strategy of deterrence, with its emphasis on massive nuclear retaliation, left statesmen on the horns of a dilemma. They could retaliate and risk Armageddon, or they could do nothing and suffer defeat. Neither option had much to recommend it, and both sides sought alternatives which would give their statesmen better choices than 'suicide' or 'surrender'. . . .

Developing Complex Defences

The stability of mutual deterrence was threatened most dramatically in the 1980s by developments in anti-ballistic missile (ABM) technology. ABMs were dangerous because by destroying intercontinental ballistic missiles (ICBMs), they reduced retaliatory capability and therefore undermined the vulnerability on which the entire edifice of deterrence was built. Worries about this technology had surfaced in the late 1960s, but at that time the genie was put back in the bottle by the 1972 ABM treaty which, with minor exceptions, prohibited the deployment of these missiles by either side. In 1983, when President [Ronald] Reagan outlined his 'Strategic Defense Initiative' it looked as if the bottle was about to be uncorked once more. American scientists began to explore the possibility of building a very complicated 'Star Wars' defence sys-

1. The military, political, and ideological barrier established between the Soviet bloc and Western Europe from 1945 to 1990.

tem,[2] which if deployed in its most comprehensive form, would not so much have undermined mutual deterrence, as actually replaced it with a strategy of 'mutual defence'.

It was a revolutionary idea and, theoretically at least, not without merit. If it had been implemented it would have revolutionised nuclear strategy and ended the era of mutual deterrence. However, for a variety of reasons, not least the difficulties associated with the new exotic space-based surveillance and interceptor systems, research was put on the back burner. Evidence mounted that the new systems were bound to be horrendously expensive and might ultimately be technically flawed.

And so 'mutual deterrence' survived. However, the concerns which had prompted President Reagan to seek some other path to security were shared by many people outside the defence community. It seemed preposterous that a superpower should base its security on the vulnerability of its own people and a threat which, if implemented, would probably destroy life as we know it. The flaws in 'mutual deterrence' were widely appreciated. It assumed an unjustifiable level of rationality on the part of statesmen; it failed to address the problems of war caused by human error, mechanical failures in weapons systems, false alarms, miscalculations, accidents, etc. Clearly, 'mutual deterrence' did not make war between the superpowers impossible—only less likely. Reducing the incidence of war is an important achievement, but the failure to reduce it to zero meant that sooner or later deterrence would fail, and when it failed the ensuing war would be much more destructive than if the belligerents had not acquired the massive arsenals necessary for mutual deterrence.

Examining the Criticism

Some of the most serious criticisms of the strategy focused on the question of 'credibility'. Few doubted that the US had the physical capability to devastate the USSR, but did she have the will to retaliate? Two reasons were advanced for thinking there was some doubt about the matter. First, because the United States would be

2. Because the defense system President Reagan proposed was meant to destroy missiles from space, it became known as "Star Wars," after a popular science fiction movie.

faced with the decision to retaliate only when the strategy of mutual deterrence had failed. What, said the critics, is the point of executing a threat when the whole point of making it in the first place was to avoid being put in the position of having to carry it out? Second, what is the point of a retaliatory strike which, if implemented, would provoke a further round of attacks and leave the US in an even worse mess than it was already in? In some circumstances retaliation would be tantamount to suicide, and for that reason the threat to engage in it is not very plausible. At the end of the day, as Robert McNamara once pointed out, 'You cannot fashion a credible deterrent out of an incredible act'. . . .

It was not just the military weaknesses of the strategy which critics latched on to. They pointed out that deterrence fostered a biased, conflict-orientated view of the world, and brainwashed society with the language and imagery of violence. Over the years the deterrent strategists promoted a climate in which war—even nuclear war—became psychologically acceptable. It deadened the sensibilities of millions of people by accustoming them to 'thinking about the unthinkable'. Furthermore, deterrence belittled the possibilities of disarmament and underplayed the importance of politics and diplomacy in resolving the problems of East-West relations. Instead of trying to remove the causes of tension, deterrent strategists tackled the problem of peace and security by trying to make the consequences of war so bad that nobody would dare fight. Instead of devising imaginative policies to end the Cold War, Western leaders were anaesthetised by a strategy which seemed to offer peace—albeit uneasy peace—with no political effort whatsoever. In this respect mutual deterrence was a comforting philosophy, but by imposing a military solution on what was fundamentally a political problem it was a misconceived strategy. Its effect was to stultify diplomacy, and keep American and Western foreign policy in a tense straightjacket for thirty years.

No Alternative

To be fair, many of the nuclear strategists who had articulated and supported the philosophy of mutual deterrence were fully aware of its weaknesses. They accepted it not because it was ideal but because they could see no alternative. It was the 'least bad' solution to the problems of the nuclear age and the Cold War.

Evaluating this strategy is not easy, if only because it is impossible to prove a connection between the absence of war and the threat made to deter it. It is much easier to point to the things which mutual deterrence did not do during the Cold War. It did not diminish East-West conflict; it did not halt the arms race; it did not prevent a whole series of international crises—from Berlin to Cuba; nor did it prevent Soviet adventurism in the Third World.

However, what cannot be disputed is that despite ideological rivalry and political hostility, war between the superpowers did not occur, and common sense suggests that the possession of overwhelming nuclear capability by both sides probably had something to do with it. After all, there is something terribly persuasive about a nuclear missile pointing down your throat, and even before deterrence became 'mutual' and 'stable' the prospect of thermonuclear war must have induced a mood of caution on both sides. There is plenty of evidence, for example, that during the Cuban Missile Crisis, the fear of nuclear war caused both sides to pull back from the brink. Another way in which this caution manifested itself was in the determination of both superpowers to avoid direct physical conflict and the dangers of escalation which would be inherent in even low level wars between them. During the Cold War years both the United States and the Soviet Union were involved in a number of major wars—from Korea in 1950, to Afghanistan in 1979, but they were careful not to tread too heavily on each other's toes.

Now that the Cold War is history and the long shadow of nuclear war has been lifted, deterrence seems to have lost some of its relevance. Nevertheless, it remains a foundation stone in the defence policies of both the United States and Russia, and it features equally prominently in the military policies of all the nuclear powers, including Britain. Although the international scene has been transformed since 1989, the pervasive logic which convinced a generation of post-war strategists may yet convince the next generation.

Viewpoint 2

"The strategy of deterrence was self-defeating; it provoked the kind of behavior it was designed to prevent."

Nuclear Deterrence Was a Counterproductive Cold War Strategy

Richard Ned Lebow and Janice Gross Stein

According to Richard Ned Lebow and Janice Gross Stein in the following viewpoint, nuclear deterrence fueled the arms race and increased tension between the United States and the Soviet Union. Indeed, nuclear deterrence provoked rather than restrained the two superpowers. For example, in the early years of the Cold War, the authors maintain, President John F. Kennedy's boasts of nuclear superiority prompted Soviet premier Nikita Khrushchev to install missiles in Cuba to protect Soviet interests there. Nuclear deterrence was not necessary to prevent major hostilities between the superpowers; in fact, confrontation between them had declined once both established spheres of influence in Europe. In retrospect, the Cold War policy of nuclear deterrence was not only unnecessary to prevent war but

Richard Ned Lebow and Janice Gross Stein, "Five Lessons from the Cold War," *Technology Review*, vol. 98, August/September 1995, pp. 69–72. Copyright © 1995 by the Association of Alumni and Alumnae of MIT. Reproduced by permission.

contributed to the tensions between the superpowers that made war more likely. Lebow, professor of political science at the University of Pittsburgh, and Stein, professor of conflict management at the University of Toronto, are coauthors of *We All Lost the Cold War.*

Many politicians, generals, and academic strategists assert that the U.S. nuclear arsenal restrained the Soviet Union throughout the Cold War. In reality, the strategy of deterrence was self-defeating; it provoked the kind of behavior it was designed to prevent.

Leaders on both sides recognized that only a madman would use nuclear weapons against a nuclear adversary. They therefore tried, and to a disturbing degree succeeded in, convincing the other that they might be sufficiently out of control to implement their threats. Each consequently became less secure, more threatened, and less confident of the robust reality of deterrence. While fear of nuclear war made leaders inwardly cautious, their public posturing convinced their adversaries that they were aggressive, risk-prone, and even irrational.

Newly declassified documents and extensive interviews with Soviet and U.S. officials have permitted us to reconstruct the deliberations of leaders of both superpowers before, during, and after the two most serious nuclear confrontations of the last 30 years: the Cuban Missile Crisis of 1962, which led President [John F.] Kennedy and Soviet Premier [Nikita] Khrushchev to the brink of nuclear war; and the 1973 Middle East War, where the Soviet Union's threat to intervene on behalf of Egypt led the United States to put its nuclear forces on full alert. Our evaluation of these events suggests five conclusions about the political role of nuclear weapons:

1. Attempts to exploit real or imagined nuclear advantages for political gain usually fail.

During the late 1950s and early 1960s, Khrushchev and Kennedy tried to intimidate each other with claims of strategic superiority. Both efforts backfired. Khrushchev's threats and boasts strengthened Western resolve to hold the line in Berlin and prompted Kennedy to initiate a major strategic buildup.[1] Kennedy's threats against Cuba, his assertions of strategic superiority, and his deployment of Jupiter missiles in Turkey—all intended to dissuade Khrushchev from challenging the West in Berlin—instead convinced Khrushchev that he needed to fortify Cuba with missiles to prevent a U.S. invasion and to compensate for Soviet strategic inferiority. Both leaders were willing to risk a serious confrontation to avoid creating the impression of weakness or irresolution.

2. *A threat to use nuclear weapons lacks credibility.*

The destructiveness of nuclear weapons makes nuclear threats more frightening but less believable—especially when those threats are directed against adversaries who have the capability to retaliate in kind.

During the [Cuban] missile crisis, for example, Khrushchev believed that Kennedy was too rational to start a nuclear war. He worried instead that foreign-policy hawks would push Kennedy into attacking Cuba with conventional forces, and that armed clashes between the invading Americans and the Soviet forces on the island committed to Cuba's defense would escalate into a wider and perhaps uncontrollable war.

In 1973, the American nuclear alert had even less influence on the Soviet leadership. [Soviet premier Leonid] Brezhnev and his advisers did not believe that the interests at stake for either the United States or the Soviet Union justified war, and concluded that the U.S. alert was an attempt to divert the U.S. public's attention from the Watergate scandal[2] that was beginning to engulf [Richard Nixon's] presidency.

---

1. The city of Berlin was located in Soviet-occupied East Germany. The United States, Great Britain, and France were determined to remain in West Berlin and to maintain their legal right of free access to that city. On August 30, 1961, President Kennedy ordered National Guardsmen and reservists to active duty in response to Soviet moves to cut off Allied access to Berlin. East Germans, stirred by the crisis, fled to West Berlin in increasing numbers. The construction of the Berlin Wall on August 13, 1961, effectively sealed off the best escape route open to disenchanted East Germans, thus halting the mass movement of people to the West.   2. Watergate was a series of scandals occurring during the Nixon administration in which members of the executive branch organized illegal political espionage against their perceived opponents and were charged with violation of the public trust, bribery, contempt of Congress, and attempted obstruction of justice for trying to cover up their involvement.

3. Nuclear threats are fraught with risk.

In both 1962 and 1973, U.S. leaders were uninformed about the consequences and implications of strategic alerts. In 1973, American leaders fully understood neither the technical meaning nor the operational consequences of the "defense condition III" (DEFCON III) alert that they had ordered. They did not realize, for example, that the decision to move to DEFCON III would entail alerting U.S. nuclear forces in Europe. During the Cuban crisis, when conventional and nuclear forces were moved to an even higher level of alert, the risk of military insubordination posed a serious threat to the resolution of the crisis.

Disgruntled military officers in the Soviet Union for example, willfully misinterpreted their orders not to fire at American airplanes or ships unless Cuba was attacked. Outraged at having to tolerate American intelligence overflights of Cuba, they shot down a U-2 reconnaissance aircraft with a surface-to-air missile. The downing of this plane and the death of its pilot was arguably the most serious moment of the crisis, prompting almost unanimous agreement among the president's military advisers that he should order a retaliatory air strike. Further attacks on American aircraft would have left him little choice but to do so.

On the American side, the most serious mishap occurred on Saturday morning [October 26, 1962], at about 10:30 Washington time. An Alaska-based U-2 operated by the Strategic Air Command strayed into Soviet air space over the Chukotski Peninsula in eastern Siberia. Soviet MiG fighter jets were scrambled from a base near Wrangel Island. When the American pilot radioed for assistance, U.S. fighter aircraft armed with low-yield, nuclear air-to-air missiles were sent to escort him home. The U-2 left Soviet air space without any shots being fired.

The confrontations of 1962 and 1973 suggest that there are stark trade-offs between the political leverage that military preparations are expected to confer and the risks of inadvertent escalation they entail. American leaders showed a poor understanding of these trade-offs: they significantly overvalued the political benefit of nuclear alerts and were insensitive to their risks.

4. Strategic buildups are more likely to provoke than to restrain adversaries.

Khrushchev thought that the West behaved cautiously in the 1950s because of a growing respect for the economic as well as military power of the socialist camp. Therefore, more visible demonstrations of Soviet power in the form of nuclear threats and missile deployments would strengthen the hands of "sober realists" in Washington who favored accommodation with the Soviet Union.

But Khrushchev's initiatives had the opposite effect: by intensifying American fears of Soviet intentions and capabilities, they strengthened the position of anti-Soviet militants. In fact, Kennedy's warnings to Khrushchev not to deploy missiles in Cuba, and the subsequent U.S. blockade, were largely a response to the growing domestic political pressures to act decisively against the Soviet Union and its Cuban ally.

Brezhnev, expecting that Soviet nuclear capabilities would prevent the United States from engaging in nuclear blackmail, continued to accumulate warheads and missiles. But U.S. officials, who had believed that the Soviet Union would stop its strategic buildup once it had achieved parity with the United States, were troubled. The Soviet strategic spending appeared to confirm the predictions of militants in Washington that Moscow's goal was strategic superiority, even a first-strike capability (that is, enough weapons to cripple in one blow the other side's retaliatory force). The Brezhnev buildup, along with the Soviet invasion of Afghanistan [in 1979], helped Republicans to defeat President [Jimmy] Carter and the SALT [Strategic Arms Limitation Talks] II agreement, and provided the Reagan administration with justification for massive arms spending.

U.S. attempts to put pressure on the Soviet Union through arms buildups were equally counterproductive. By the time [Mikhail] Gorbachev became general secretary in 1985, he was deeply committed to fundamental change in Soviet foreign policy and determined to overhaul an economy crippled by defense spending and, more importantly, by structural rigidities. Gorbachev felt free to propose deep cuts in nuclear weapons because he was confident that the United States would not attack the Soviet Union. Because he saw no threat of a U.S. attack, Gorbachev was not intimidated by the Reagan administration's military program. Alexander Yakovlev, one of Gorbachev's closet advisers, insists that Reagan's commitment to the Strategic Defense Initiative only made it more difficult for Gorbachev to persuade his officials that arms control and an end to the Cold War was in the Soviet interest. The Cold War ended in spite of Ronald Reagan's arms buildup, not because of it.

5. *Nuclear deterrence is robust when leaders on both sides fear war and are aware of each other's fears.*

More important than the balance of nuclear capabilities, or leaders' estimates of relative nuclear advantage, is their judgment of an adversary's intentions. The Cuban Missile Crisis was a turning point in Soviet-American relations because it convinced Kennedy and Khrushchev that their adversary was just as committed as they were to avoiding nuclear war. This mutually acknowledged fear of war made the other side's nuclear capabilities less threatening and paved the way for arms-control agreements.

Not all U.S. and Soviet leaders shared this interpretation. Large segments of the national security elites of both superpowers continued to regard their adversary as implacably hostile and willing to use nuclear weapons. Brezhnev and Nixon both cited the need to deter enemy attack to justify continuing buildups in their countries' strategic forces. Western militants did not begin to change their estimate of Soviet intentions until Gorbachev made clear his commitment to ending the arms race and the Cold War.

Kirk. © 1992 by Kirk Anderson. Reprinted with permission.

Deterrence in Hindsight

The Cold War began as Soviet-American competition in Central Europe in the aftermath of Germany's defeat. Once recognized spheres of influence were established, however, confrontations between the superpowers in the heart of Europe diminished; even Berlin ceased to be a flashpoint once the superpowers reached an understanding about the two Germanies.

By the 1970s, the growing arsenal and ever-more-accurate weapons of mass destruction that each superpower aimed at the other had become the primary source of mutual insecurity and tension. Moscow and Washington no longer argued about the status quo in Europe but about the new weapons systems each deployed to threaten the other.

Since the late 1960s, when the Soviet Union developed an effective retaliatory arsenal, both superpowers have had to live with nuclear vulnerability. Some leaders in both countries advocated development of the ability to launch a preemptive strike, ballistic missile defense systems, or other illusory visions of security in a nuclear world. But nuclear vulnerability could not be eliminated. Mutually assured destruction was a reality from which there was no escape short of political accommodation and far-reaching arms control.

The nuclear arms paradox resembles that often found in medicine. The same chemotherapy drugs that control cancer can also kill the patient. Arsenic, in controlled doses, can treat such diseases as syphilis and schistosomiasis. The outcome depends on the virulence of the disease, how early the disease is detected, the amount of drugs administered, and the resistance of the patient to both the disease and the cure.

So it is with nuclear deterrence. To a certain extent, deterrence is stabilizing because it prompts mutual caution. Too much deterrence, or deterrence applied inappropriately to a frightened and vulnerable adversary, can fuel an arms race that makes both sides less secure and provokes the aggression it is designed to prevent. As with any medicine, the key to successful deterrence is to administer the proper dosage.

Viewpoint 3

"America felt obliged by Cold War pressures to live up to its democratic and civil libertarian ideals."

The Cold War Advanced Democratic Ideals in the United States

Arch Puddington

Claims by American liberals that the United States sacrificed civil liberties during the Cold War are erroneous, argues Arch Puddington in the following viewpoint. In fact, Puddington maintains, because the United States was the leader of the free world during the Cold War, it was driven to promote democratic ideals, particularly at home. By focusing on the early years of the Cold War, during which the civil liberties of a few left-leaning Americans were curtailed, scholars of the American left ignore advances in civil rights and improvements in the economic status of America's working class that occurred during the Cold War. For example, Puddington asserts, during the Korean and Vietnam Wars, the U.S. military became integrated, and blacks in the military obtained positions of authority. Moreover, he claims, union leaders who opposed communism helped America's working class be the first to obtain middle-class status dur-

Arch Puddington, "Good Times," *Heterodoxy*, vol. 7, February 1999, pp. 4–5. Copyright © 1999 by *Heterodoxy*. Reproduced by permission.

ing the Cold War. Puddington also claims that the Cold War led to positive changes in immigration policies, such as allowing Asians to immigrate to America. American universities also benefited during the Cold War as the government channelled money to scholars working on projects that might help the United States win the Cold War. Puddington is vice president for research at Freedom House, an organization that advances democratic values and opposes dictatorships worldwide.

To its many critics, the Cold War stands as the low point of American history. World War II may be recalled as the good fight against fascism and dictatorship. The Depression may be remembered as a time when the poor drew comfort from FDR [U.S. president Franklin D. Roosevelt], the New Deal, an activist government and a vibrant, progressive political movement. But the Cold War summons up no similar images to inspire or reassure. To moderate critics of the era, the essence of the matter was summed up in an episode of CNN's documentary series on the Cold War, in which McCarthyism and Stalinism[1] are portrayed as morally equivalent evils. To more ideologically driven opponents, the Cold War was a time when fear and repression dominated American political life, a sterile conformity defined American culture, and a "national security state" weakened and undermined one after another of our democratic institutions.

The Cold War at Home

The controversy over the Cold War's domestic implications rages even as the debate over Communism's merits has been laid to rest. . . . For the left, the real issue is not McCarthyism, but anti-Communism itself. And similarly with the left's ongoing attempt

1. McCarthyism is the act of unscrupulously accusing people of disloyalty, for example, claiming they are Communists; it is also the time period during the Cold War when Senator Joe McCarthy made such accusations. McCarthy often ruined careers based on flimsy evidence and unidentified informers. Stalinism is a form of government in which the ruler is an absolute dictator who is not restricted by a constitution or laws and is associated with the government led by Soviet premier Joseph Stalin.

to rewrite the history of the domestic impact of the Cold War. As leftist critics are well aware, the period of the "Great Fear"—with its House Un-American Activities Committee hearings, loyalty oaths, and blacklists—was relatively brief, lasting from 1947 to the mid-Fifties. The case against the Cold War, however, encompasses the entire period of U.S.- Soviet rivalry, from the postwar takeover of Eastern Europe to the fall of the Berlin Wall. It asserts that the Cold War not only threatened our civil liberties, but distorted our civic values, set back the cause of civil rights, weakened organized labor, had a corrupting influence on the university, damaged civil liberties, created an economy dependent on military spending, and prevented the emergence of genuine political alternatives to the dominant capitalist system.

On almost every point, the critics of Cold War America are wrong. The Cold War was not a period of reactionary ascendancy, but rather one in which liberal values usually prevailed. Occasionally, liberal ideas won out in part as a reaction to McCarthyite excess. More often, liberal ideas advanced because America felt obliged by Cold War pressures to live up to its democratic and civil libertarian ideals.

Racial Gains

Thus, while many factors led to the triumph of the civil rights movement, one consideration was the American political leadership's embarrassment at racial segregation at a time when the U.S. was competing for the hearts and minds of the world's non-white people. The civil rights agenda did not win adoption because of Cold War calculations, but the Cold War probably accelerated the pace of change.

The left, of course, sees things differently, ascribing the persecution of Martin Luther King and other civil rights leaders to the anti-Communist paranoia of J. Edgar Hoover and other government officials. Hoover certainly hated Communism and detested King. But his animus towards King derived from many sources, not the least of which was the FBI chief's dislike for race-mixing. In the absence of the Communist question, Hoover would have found some other justification for his anti-King vendetta.

Ironically, some of the earliest and most far-reaching racial gains occurred in that ultimate Cold War institution, the American military. It was during the Korean War that military units, at President [Harry] Truman's insistence, were first integrated, a development which inspired the civil rights movement to seek broader changes in civilian society. And it was during Vietnam and after that black military men began to achieve positions of authority throughout the military services.

Improving Immigration Policies

Changes in American immigration law were also motivated in part by sensitivities over America's Cold War image, as the commitment to eliminate racial discrimination in our domestic life led inevitably to a decision to purge our immigration policies of ethnic or racial bias. The debate which preceded adoption of immigration reform legislation in 1965 made frequent reference to the hypocrisy of America's claiming leadership of the Free World while maintaining immigration policies which discriminated against Asians. [Former Speaker of the House] Tip O'Neill summed up a commonly held view when he declared that the restrictive policy "presents the ironic situation in which we are willing to send our American youth to aid these people [the Vietnamese] in their struggle against Communist aggression while at the same time we are indicating that they are not good enough to be Americans."

The results of the 1965 changes have been a revolution in immigration's racial composition. Where previously immigration was overwhelmingly made up of Europeans, it is today dominated by immigrants from Latin America and Asia, non-white and often non-Christian groups which were once excluded or, if they were permitted to immigrate, treated poorly once they arrived. Furthermore, the Cold War policy of automatically granting asylum to refugees from Communism primarily benefited Cubans, Vietnamese, Cambodians, and other non-Europeans. It is thus indisputable that the status of non-whites improved, in some cases dramatically, during and in part due to the Cold War.

The Labor Unions

But what of organized labor? In her recent study of the domestic impact of McCarthyism, *Many Are the Crimes*, Ellen Schrecker claims that McCarthyism and the Cold War had a devastating effect on the trade union movement. The purge of Communist-led unions by the CIO [Congress of Industrial Organizations], she contends, cost labor its dynamism and contributed to its eventual decline. "The anticommunist crusade," Schrecker writes, "diverted the mainstream unions from organizing the unorganized." She also blames the Cold War for making labor "more centralized, corrupt, and distant from its members."

The truth is that during much of the Cold War the American working man and his union fared extremely well. Unions enjoyed high concentrations of membership in the basic industries throughout the non-South; at their height in the mid-Fifties, unions represented some 35 percent of the private work force and a higher proportion outside the Southern states. Union members also made important economic gains; the American working class became the first working class in history to enter the ranks of the middle class. During the 1960s, unions gained hundreds of thousands of new members after scoring major organizing breakthroughs in the public sector.

Schrecker and other critics do not blame the labor movement's subsequent decline on the Cold War per se. Instead, they advance the argument that labor forfeited its independence, militance, and fighting spirit when it accepted the terms of the Cold War consensus and abandoned the struggle to bring about significant changes in American capitalism. While labor prospered when times were good, it was unable to mount a concerted counteroffensive against the ruinous impact of economic globalization and technological change.

Communists in the Labor Movement

The left's version of American history is littered with "if only's." The claim that Smokestack America and its millions of well-compensated, unionized jobs could have been salvaged "if only" the labor movement had adopted a class warfare stance, and welcomed the participation of Communists and other radicals, is no more convincing than the belief that American politics would have moved in a more radical direction if only the left had founded an independent party based on the labor movement, racial minorities, and militant feminists.

Of course, organized labor represents government workers, teachers, well-paid construction workers, airline pilots, and professional athletes, groups that are hardly likely to remain associated with an institution which adopts an adversarial stance towards the American economic system. As for the supposition that Communists might have played an important role in a revitalized labor movement, a look at the European experience suggests the absurdity of that argument. The English example is particularly worthy of note. There, Communists, pro-Communists, and assorted other radicals maintained a power base in the trade union movement right up to the 1980s. The labor movement in Great Britain was the most militant and class-conscious in the democratic world, and its effects on the English economy were nothing short of ruinous. Ultimately, aggressive trade unionism did bring a realignment of British politics—a realignment to the right, embodied in the governments of Margaret Thatcher and the transformation of the Labour Party under Tony Blair.

Communists still retain a major role in the French labor movement, one of Europe's weakest. On the other hand, Communists play no role in the labor movements of Germany and Scandinavia, where unions continue to represent high proportions of the work force and exert a strong—too strong, some would say—influence over economic policy.

A Commitment to Ideals

Nor do George Meany, Lane Kirkland, David Dubinsky, and other anti-Communist labor leaders have any apologies to make for their commitment to America's triumph in the Cold War. More than anything, it is American labor's patriotism that infuriates and perplexes the left.

In fact, labor's support for the Cold War derived from sound practical motives. To begin with, labor's blue-collar membership was strongly anti-Communist, as were non-union workers whom labor hoped to organize. Another consideration was labor's unpleasant experiences with Communist-led factionalism in a number of unions, including the United Auto Workers (UAW).

Labor also saw Communism as an economic threat insofar as

Communist regimes destroyed free trade unions and replaced them with labor associations under the total control of the party-state. American trade unionists, in fact, regarded the Communist union model as particularly sinister precisely because it claimed to speak in the interest of the working class. The AFL-CIO [American Federation of Labor/Congress of Industrial Organizations] feared that countries under Communist control might, under conditions of détente, succeed in luring American investment and the transfer of American jobs through policies which kept unions tame and wages low. American union leaders thus opposed Communist unions for much the same reason they today oppose American investment in low-wage countries where union rights are suppressed.

American Civil Liberties

A cornerstone of the left's brief is the contention that Cold War hysteria and security mania led to a massive assault on civil liberties and a reign of terror against ordinary American citizens. To advance this argument, of course, it is necessary to restrict the definition of the Cold War to its earliest years, the period between 1947, when Truman initiated his loyalty program, to the end of the McCarthy era in the mid-Fifties. Even during that benighted period, the "reign of terror" was limited to Americans with past or present Communist connections and a few affiliated with non-Communist radical groupings. As for the loyalty oaths, anti-subversive legislation, and McCarthyite bullying, the principal lesson is that the American commitment to civil liberties and individual rights reasserted itself rather quickly. McCarthyism's most important lingering effect is in its having given the left a blunt weapon to wield against the American system. In books, magazines, movies, documentaries, in works of art, we are reminded *ad nauseam* about America's failure to live up to its democratic ideals, with the message, often explicitly stated, that a McCarthyite revival, or something much worse, is always a possibility.

The left has a certain difficulty in accounting for the state of civil liberties in the post-McCarthy period. America continued to fight Communism, and yet the country underwent an explosion of rights—individual rights, group rights, cultural freedoms. The rights of press and assembly were expanded, public employees gained the right to join unions and engage in collective bargaining, women and minorities gained equality under the law, criminal defendants won the right to an attorney and a series of procedural protections against abusive—and not so abusive—police tactics.

Americans supported most civil liberties changes—the main exception being court decisions which were seen as handcuffing the police—because they generally believed in an expansive definition of personal liberties. These radical changes occurred, bear in mind, when the Cold War raged as intensely as it did during its earliest years, a period which included a major war in Southeast Asia, several minor conflicts which involved American troops, U.S.-Soviet competition in the development of lethal weapons systems, nuclear war alerts, and an increasingly angry debate over America's role in the world. In fact, in many respects, America has become more conservative since the Cold War's end.

The Impact on American Universities

No institution of American society was said to have been more thoroughly corrupted by the Cold War than the American university. Central to the New Left's ideology was the proposition that students comprised an oppressed class, much like blacks. According to this line of reasoning, the university had abandoned its core educational mission by permitting itself to be exploited for Cold War related research and by shaping its priorities around Cold War security needs. In so doing so, student activists charged, university officials allowed national security considerations to distort curriculum, neglected teaching in favor of research, and inculcated a dehumanized environment inhospitable to human relations and genuine learning.

A particularly helpful source in reassessing the Cold War's impact on the university is, ironically, a product of anti–Cold War, revisionist scholarship. *The Cold War and the University* is a two-volume series of essays which delves into the Cold War's alleged impact on everything from English language studies to the earth sciences. The essays are written from a decidedly leftist perspective, and contributors include such radical venerables as Noam Chomsky, Howard Zinn, and Christopher Simpson. Some, however, are written by thoughtful and more moderate scholars, in particular several scientists who provide some worthy antidotes to the usual leftist cliches.

Support for Universities

As these essays make clear, the Cold War's most important effect on higher education was to involve the federal government for the first time as a major source of funding for the university. With the U.S.-Soviet rivalry heavily dependent on scientific and military technological development, the government ploughed billions of dollars into university research programs, and while the bulk was directed towards the hard sciences, funds were also made available for the social sciences and the liberal arts as well.

All this was to usher in a golden era for university faculty. The need for professors was constantly growing, creating opportunities for advancement and higher pay for just about everyone, history professors as well as nuclear physicists. Conditions were especially good for young scholars, who in pre–Cold War days had often labored in semi-poverty until tenure was attained. Now they were the beneficiaries of doctoral fellowships, grants-in-aid, and a guaranteed job with tenure track upon graduation. Having secured a position, a scholar might well receive a federal research grant, or a contract to conduct research paid for by a private corporation. In some cases, the research might have specific application to the military, the space program, or some other government priority. Often, however, the government and even some corporations would support basic research whose military use was not at all clear, and might not be determined for years to come.

As for repression, after the initial wave of McCarthyism few university professors lost their jobs for participation in antigovernment protest movements. A.C. Lewontin, a professor of biology at Harvard, notes that throughout the Sixties he was active in anti-Vietnam causes, worked on a collaborative project with Vietnamese Communists, gave public speeches against the war, and even submitted a research grant proposal to the North Vietnamese government. While Lewontin was under FBI surveillance during this period, he continued to work under contract on projects for the Atomic Energy Commission and the Department of Energy.

What accounts for the left's intellectual obtuseness? Part of the explanation can be traced to the left's abiding faith in the socialist idea. The left understood that while America was officially open to non-Communist forms of socialism, in fact real socialism—as opposed to the watered-down social democratic variant—would inevitably resemble Communism in most important details. Nicaraguan socialism under the Sandinistas was in many respects similar to Cuban socialism under Castro, which itself was barely distinguishable from the Soviet variety. Likewise, while America during the Cold War was dominated by liberal values, it was thoroughly inhospitable to any significant rearrangement of economic priorities. Michael Harrington, a one-time Cold War radical who shifted to a neutralist stance during the 1970s, argued that progress towards socialism in the U.S. was impossible as long as Cold War values prevailed, a view that was widely shared on the left.

Furthermore, where the Cold War is concerned, the left's powers of rational judgment have been distorted by the self-righteous conviction that nothing positive can be achieved unless it enjoys a "progressive" seal of approval. Under this standard, the Spanish Civil War and World War II are deemed "good" conflicts, whereas World War I and Korea are dismissed as unworthy of American intervention. And while the Cold War's *denouement* represented a catastrophic setback for the American left, the demonization of the domestic Cold War has been largely successful, if only because the left has largely had the field to itself. . . . The terms of the controversy changed only after scholars like [Harvey] Klehr and [Ronald] Radosh issued a direct challenge to the prevailing dogma that was fortified by dogged research and a shrewd grasp of the dynamics of radical politics. Although their findings still meet with resistance, their conclusions have succeeded in puncturing the myth of American Communists as nothing more than progressive-thinking men and women who supported trade unions and fought for racial justice. A similar examination of the Cold War's effect on American democracy would no doubt result in the destruction of the left's most cherished remaining myth, that the United States is a country where fear and reaction once prevailed, and the potential for a domestic police state still exists.

Viewpoint 4

"The United States has paid dearly for its Cold War victory and for the satisfaction of creating the foundations of the Cold War order."

The Cold War Was Unnecessary and Costly for the United States

Richard J. Barnet

In the following viewpoint Richard J. Barnet reexamines two documents written in the beginning of the Cold War: George F. Kennan's 1947 article "The Sources of Soviet Conflict," written under the pseudonym Mr. X, and journalist Walter Lippmann's book *The Cold War*, which consisted of columns written in response to Kennan's article. Kennan's article was the inspiration for the U.S. policy of containment of Soviet aggression. According to Barnet, Kennan maintained that although the Soviet Union was at that time ideologically and economically weak, it was committed to proving the superiority of the Communist philosophy. In Barnet's view, President Harry Truman exaggerated Kennan's portrayal of the Soviets as unshakeable in their desire for world domination in order to win support for the pol-

Richard J. Barnet, "A Balance Sheet: Lippmann, Kennan, and the Cold War," *Diplomatic History*, vol. 302, Spring 1992. Copyright © 1992 by Blackwell Publishers. Reproduced by permission.

icy of containment. If Truman had considered the actual weaknesses of the Soviet Union at that time, he might have adopted Lippmann's strategy—to encourage, through diplomacy, the demobilization of Soviet forces in Europe—instead. Had Lippmann's strategy rather than Kennan's been implemented the Cold War could have been prevented, Barnet maintains. Truman did not heed Lippmann's advice, however, and the Cold War resulted in a hollow victory for the United States. As Lippmann correctly predicted, the enormous costs of fighting the war left the United States economically and morally exhausted, Barnet claims. Barnet is a senior fellow and former codirector of the Institute for Policy Studies, a research institute known for its criticism of U.S. Cold War policy. Barnet's books include *Global Dreams*, *The Rockets' Red Glare*, and *The Youngest Minds*.

R e-reading, [renowned journalist] Walter Lippmann's columns on George Kennan's [1947] "X" article forty-three years after they were first published . . . is an unsettling experience. What are we to make of these twelve columns that Lippmann published a few months later as *The Cold War*? The clarity, the intellectual power, and the breadth of the analysis cannot fail to impress the reader, whatever one thinks of Lippmann's argument. As the United States stands on the threshold of another series of fateful choices, the contemporary relevance of the Lippmann-Kennan debate is striking. . . .

Kennan's Predictions

The disintegration of the Soviet system came about exactly in the way that Kennan had predicted. The system contained the seeds of its own destruction. The expensive pursuit of military equivalence no doubt accelerated the process, and for this the United States can take some dubious credit for hooking the Soviets into a spending race that was more precipitously disastrous for the Soviet system than for American society and its economic base. But the Cold War also helped to strengthen the hard-line leadership. Indeed, some reformist historians in the former Soviet Union believe that an earlier readiness of the United States to negotiate with

Stalin's successors, or even with Stalin, over the fate of Europe would have caused the winds of change to blow earlier, harder, and faster, and that some Soviet leader might well have taken the risks of *perestroika* in the 1950s or the 1960s. Who knows? But as Kennan noted, the myth of capitalist encirclement was an important Stalinist weapon of social control. Beginning in the late 1940s, the extravagant rhetoric of officials, generals, and politicians in the United States about the inevitability of war with the Soviet Union—and the need to get it over with before the year of maximum danger arrived—served to confirm Stalinist paranoia and to reinforce the climate of fear on which the dictator built his regime. The hostility of the West also served to explain to two Soviet generations why the workers' government could not deliver on its promises to the workers.

But George Kennan neither predicted nor advocated a military victory, not even one that rested on a spending race and the demonstration of superior technological prowess. He has spent the second half of his life explaining away his "X" article, apologizing for its excessively militaristic ring and lamenting the uses to which it was put. Yet, it was Kennan's eloquent distillations of his complex, contradictory thought (backed by a reputation for expertise on the Soviet Union that few could match)—in such phrases as the "adroit and vigilant application of counter-force," or "the Russians look forward to a duel of infinite duration," or the emphasis on the Soviets' "neurotic view of world affairs," or the "instinctive Russian sense of insecurity"—that took official Washington by storm in early 1946. The picture that emerged from Kennan's analysis was of an ambitious power in the grip of an irrational ideology and impervious to conventional diplomacy. His "Long Telegram" was leaked to *Time* a year before the "X" article appeared, and his message was amplified and distorted as a brief for policies that he never supported, and indeed would at a much later stage publicly oppose. . . .

The Case for Negotiation

Lippmann is unwilling to assume that the "neurotic world view" and the totalitarian organization of Stalinist society meant that the Soviet Union was so inexorably committed to an expansionist course as to be beyond the influence of adroit diplomacy. Given the obvious Soviet weakness that Kennan identified, why was it so clearly impossible for the most powerful nation on earth to press the heirs of the Russian empire to accept a settlement?

> I am contending that the American diplomatic effort should be concentrated on the problem created by the armistice— which is on how the continent of Europe can be evacuated by the three non-European armies which are now inside Europe. This is the problem which will have to be solved if the independence of the European nations is to be restored. Without that there is no possibility of a tolerable peace. But if these armies withdraw, there will be a very different balance of power in the world than there is today, and one which cannot easily be upset. For the nations of Europe, separately and in groups, perhaps even in unity, will then, and then only, cease to be the stakes and the pawns of the Russian-American conflict.

It is hard to read the "X" article and come to any conclusion about when negotiation with the Soviet Union would make sense, if ever. Read literally, the article seems to say that there could be no useful diplomacy until the mellowing process was well advanced. We know that Kennan had misgivings about the division of Germany, German rearmament, and the deployment of NATO [North Atlantic Treaty Organization] armies beyond the temporary "modest shield" behind which Western Europe would recover its economic and political stability. He was appalled by the global pretensions of the Truman Doctrine.[1] But no one could guess it from the cold print that was so effectively used to support all of these policies.

An Alternative Course

Lippmann attacked Kennan for not keeping his eye on "the material cause and reason of the conflict," which was the future of Germany and the military balance in Europe. The columnist appears

1. the policy of President Truman, as advocated in his address to Congress on March 12, 1947, to provide military and economic aid to Greece and Turkey and, by extension, to any country threatened by communism or any totalitarian ideology

more pragmatic and hardheaded than the suddenly famous diplomat. If Kennan was right that communism was already a weakening ideology and that the economic foundations of Soviet power were shaky, then the only reason that this underdeveloped country should have been considered a serious political rival was the presence of the Red Army in the middle of Europe. Given the uniquely dominant role of the United States in the world economy and its unique strength as the only big power not crippled by the war, not to mention the attraction its democratic system held for the entire war-shattered world—even Ho Chi Minh [founder and leader of the Vietnamese Communist movement] was celebrating Washington and Jefferson in 1945—why did the Truman administration not set as its overriding policy objective the redeployment and demobilization of Stalin's land forces and the avoidance of a nuclear arms race? For it was only in the military sphere that the Soviet Union had the chance to be a serious rival to the United States, and as Lippmann points out, a deal with the Soviet Union to withdraw and demobilize their forces in Europe would be largely self-verifying. Such an agreement would provide little employment "for the dialecticians, the ideologists, the sophists, and the causists" who were then building political careers on the murky text of the Yalta accords [agreements made shortly before the end of World War II between Franklin Roosevelt, Winston Churchill, and Joseph Stalin on how to proceed in the postwar world]. Soviet disengagement "is not a matter which can be hidden behind an iron curtain. It is a matter of plain and quite obvious fact."

Lippmann makes a strong case. A German settlement and withdrawal of the armies would "divide the Red Army from the Red International." It would avoid the "continual and complicated intervention" of the United States in the affairs of its allies and would spare the effort and expense of "recruiting, subsidizing, and supporting a heterogeneous array of satellites, clients, dependents, and puppets . . . around the perimeter of the Soviet Union." (Lippmann correctly saw these imperial roles as sources of weakness, not strength, and certainly not as the badge of pre-eminent or long-lasting power.)

Why did the United States not put Lippmann's strategy to the test? Why did the Truman administration launch its containment strategy by concentrating on the fringes of Europe—Turkey and Greece—rather than on its center? Why did it move so quickly to conclude that military pressure rather than diplomacy was the key to containing Russian power? . . .

Questioning U.S. Foreign Policy

I would suggest as an explanation four powerful political ideas that gripped the Truman administration; each reinforced the other, causing the architects of U.S. Cold War policy to reject the course that Lippmann proposed without even giving it serious consideration. The first was the notion that the atomic bomb was a "winning weapon" under the cover of which the United States could successfully challenge Soviet power at the periphery of the Eurasian land mass. The geopolitical faith that the balance of power would be decided by the control of raw materials, sea lanes, bases, and internal political developments outside of Europe caused the Truman administration to put greater emphasis on military pressure and less on diplomacy. . . .

The second idea that guided American policymakers was that Stalin was a reincarnation of Hitler, a man of boundless appetite, a barbarian whose word was worthless, and an ideologue as removed from the world of conventional politics as *Der Führer.* You could not do business with Stalin, and even to make the attempt would weaken political support for containment, giving the Soviet dictator an opportunity to divide the coalition against him and to confuse the American people.

The German Question

The third and perhaps most important strain in American official thinking that pushed Truman's advisers toward a military rather than a diplomatic strategy for dealing with the Soviet Union was concern about Germany. The fear that a Germany that was not locked in an American embrace might conclude a new Rapallo agreement[2] with the Soviet Union and that together the two land

2. Germany and the Soviet Union signed the Treaty of Rapallo in 1922 at Rapallo, Italy. The two signatories mutually canceled all pre–World War I debts and renounced war claims to territory. Germany was the first nation to recognize the Soviet Union after the Russian Revolution.

powers would attract Japan to a revived totalitarian alliance to challenge American hegemony was the driving force for the policy of partition on which NATO was founded. Within the Truman administration the distrust of Germany two years after the war was too strong to permit a deal with the Soviets based on the "neutralization" of Germany. Worse than the Red Army on the Elbe [River] was the prospect of a power vacuum in Germany. A long-term U.S. military presence on German soil would serve as the glue for the economic integration of an Atlantic community in which the leading role of the United States would be assured for years to come. The military alliance would exert a profound influence on the domestic politics of every Western European country, ensuring that their governments would remain pro-American and centrist.

The fourth and final strain was a deep concern about the volatility of U.S. public opinion. The American people were demanding demobilization and the armed forces were melting away. In 1946, one third of American exports were being financed through various programs of economic assistance. But conservatives, divining the public mood, were gearing up to block the "giveaway programs" on which the administration's economic and political strategies depended. . . . The containment strategy required that Americans believe that Stalin represented a threat to their own security. To sell Marshall Plan[3] aid the only way it could be sold, as an instrument of containment, it was important to close off avenues of hope that the problems of Europe could be settled through negotiation with Stalin. "I think it is a mistake," [then U.S. secretary of state] Dean Acheson told the Senate Foreign Relations Committee, "to believe that you can, at any time, sit down with the Russians and solve questions."

The Costs of Containment

Lippmann showed no interest in challenging Kennan on his judgments about Russia's vulnerabilities, much less on the facts the Soviet expert used as the basis for his judgments. His rejoinder

---

3. Also known as the European Recovery Program of 1948, the Marshall Plan provided $13.3 billion in economic aid to a war-devastated Europe.

rests rather on his assessment of American vulnerabilities that would be likely to develop in a long Cold War. Why, asked Lippmann, do we think that it is ordained that the Soviet Union must break its leg "while the United States grows a pair of wings to speed it on its way?" In his own way Lippmann was as prescient about what would happen to the United States as Kennan was about the fate of the Soviet Union. He was wrong about American staying power through nine administrations, but forty-three years later his columns do serve as an unheeded reminder of the extraordinary costs of containment.

Lippmann sounded like the George Kennan of the 1970s when he zeroed in on the rhapsodical coda of the "X" article. Kennan professed "a certain gratitude to a Providence which, by providing the American people with this implacable challenge [Soviet power and Stalinist ideology], has made their entire security as a nation dependent on their pulling themselves together and accepting the responsibilities of moral and political leadership that history plainly intended them to bear." Lippmann did not question the assertion that it was America's destiny to lead, but he did challenge both the definition of leadership and the strategy for exercising leadership. He was clearer about why he did not like the strategy. Would it not take "a blank check on the Treasury"? How could the American constitutional system be maintained if containment of communism became the national purpose? How would the president know when he was to intervene? Or was the idea to intervene everywhere? Either the president would be too little and too late with his application of "counterforce" or he would have to bypass the Constitution. "A policy of shifts and maneuvers may be suited to the Soviet system of government, which, as Mr. X tells us, is animated by patient persistence. It is not suited to the American system of government."

Misplaced Spending Priorities

Lippmann argues that a "free and undirected economy like our own" cannot "be used by the diplomatic planners to wage a diplomatic war against a planned economy." Forty-three years later it is tempting to say that Lippmann was wrong on this score. The "arsenal of democracy," with the world's largest GNP and the world's most formidable military force, has its problems after forty years of unrelenting military budgets, but no one at this point would exchange these difficulties for the problems in the former Soviet Union. Yet the challenge of containment caused profound changes in the American system that Lippmann feared, correctly, would be destructive. The pressures of the military competition, which was assumed in the highest reaches of the Truman administration to be the likely outcome of their policies, forced the "free and undirected economy" to develop its own planned sector; the Pentagon and the huge network of weapons procurement and maintenance facilities it fed is a market system in name only. The impact of four decades of permanent mobilization on the U.S. economy is the subject of considerable contention, but it is obvious that this mobilization transformed the nature of American capitalism—and certainly not in a direction advocated by free-market ideologues. My own view is that despite the periodic stimulus provided by cycles of military spending, military Keynesianism[4] has been a disaster, contributing to budget deficits, loss of competitive position, and the siphoning of investment funds from both public infrastructure—schools, bridges, and the like—as well as from needed industrial and technological development. The spending priorities adopted in the pursuit of containment have had a great deal to do with the decline in American economic power. Lippmann did not exactly predict this, but he raised the issue. Kennan did not. . . .

U.S. Exhaustion

After almost fifty years the Cold War struggle has destroyed the Soviet Union. In the hands of Russian, Belorussian, Ukrainian, and Kazakhstani leaders are thousands of nuclear warheads that can destroy this country, and who will gain control of them in the months ahead is by no means certain. The collapse of Soviet power and the failure of Socialist institutions open up long-term possibilities of democratic transformation. But the prospects for

---

4. Economist John Maynard Keynes advocated a policy of maintaining high employment and controlling inflation by varying the interest rates, tax rates, and public expenditure.

the immediate future may be more political upheavals and economic distress. All of this is adding to the world's immense capital needs at a moment when the United States, debt ridden and more dependent on foreign capital than at any time in [the twentieth] century, can do almost nothing to meet them. The costs of the prolonged political-military struggle that Lippmann called the Cold War can be counted not only in the neglect and deterioration of domestic institutions but also in the loss of American capacity to exercise constructive influence abroad. The world's only global military superpower lacks the material resources to maintain a competitive industrial base, the infrastructure on which a strong economy depends, or even the necessities, much less the amenities, of a good society.

How ironical it is that as Leningrad has been renamed St. Petersburg and as the seventy-five-year obsession with the Soviet Union comes to an end, the United States is now obsessed with talk of its own decline. In 1991, it once again reasserted its strength and staying power by fixing on another underdeveloped country [Iraq] against which it waged a crushing but indecisive war [the Persian Gulf War]. The United States has paid dearly for its Cold War victory and for the satisfaction of creating the foundations of the Cold War order. But the consequence—as Lippmann rightly predicted and as the last forty-three years have shown—has been political and moral exhaustion.

For Further Discussion

Chapter 1

1. Henry A. Wallace advocates seeking peace with the Soviet Union. Clark M. Clifford, on the other hand, warns against mutual agreements with Soviet leaders. How does each author's interpretation of the motivation behind Soviet conduct in Eastern Europe differ? Whose argument do you think is more dependent on the correctness of his interpretation? Explain.
2. George F. Kennan and Andrei Zhdanov both cite the ideological differences between the Soviet Union and the United States as impediments to cooperation and peace. Both see their own ideology as superior and the other's as inferior and threatening. What kind of evidence does each use to support his argument? Which author's evidence do you think is more persuasive? Explain.
3. Douglas J. Macdonald and Dale C. Copeland cite specific actions taken by the United States and the Soviet Union to support their arguments about the origins of the Cold War. Macdonald cites as evidence events after the Cold War began while Copeland cites evidence before the end of World War II and shortly thereafter. How does this difference affect the persuasiveness of each author's explanation of the origins of the Cold War? Explain, citing from the texts.
4. Macdonald and Copeland appear to have several objectives when presenting their evidence: to explain the origins of the Cold War, to assign blame for the forty-five-year conflict, and to support a theoretical position—traditionalist and postrevisionist. Does the evidence each cites more effectively achieve one objective over another? Explain.

Chapter 2

1. Douglas MacArthur claims that the war in Korea should be expanded to include an attack on Communist China while Harry S. Truman argues that the war should be limited to Korea. MacArthur was a prominent U.S. general while Truman was

president of the United States. In your opinion, how is each leader's role reflected in his argument?

2. Richard V. Allen concludes that the Soviet Union does not seek peaceful coexistence with the United States. To support his argument, Allen contends that the desire to be victorious over capitalism implies the destruction of the free world. What type of evidence does Allen provide to support this argument? Is it sufficient to persuade you that Soviet claims of wanting peaceful coexistence were false? Explain.

3. Steve Farrell argues that if the United States had been truly committed to eradicating communism, it could have won the war in Vietnam. Regis T. Sabol claims that any strategy that provoked the Chinese directly could have led to World War III. How is the evidence Farrell cites to support his viewpoint similar to or different from the evidence cited by Douglas MacArthur in his criticism of Truman's policy in Korea? Does Sabol make claims similar to or different from those made by Harry S. Truman? Do these similarities or differences influence which argument on the Vietnam War you find more persuasive? Explain.

Chapter 3

1. Henry A. Kissinger argues that nuclear arms limitation agreements will reduce the threat of nuclear war while G. Warren Nutter argues that these agreements in fact increase the threat. What evidence does each author use to support his argument? Whose argument do you find more persuasive? Explain, citing from the text.

2. What are the similarities between the arguments set forth by G. Warren Nutter (opposing the policy of détente) and those of Richard V. Allen (opposing "peaceful coexistence" with the Soviet Union)? How do their arguments differ?

3. Russian Dmitri Klimov cites American authorities to support his claim that the Strategic Defense Initiative weapons system proposed by Ronald Reagan is meant to achieve military superiority over the Soviet Union. His article was published in a Soviet military newspaper. What impact do you think his use of American sources had on those who read this newspaper? Do you think your answer would be the same if an American

writer had cited Soviet sources? Explain.

4. Raymond L. Garthoff argues that the Cold War was caused by the Soviet belief in the inevitability of conflict between communism and capitalism. He concludes that only a Soviet leader such as Mikhail Gorbachev could have changed this stance and thus ended the war. Margaret Thatcher, on the other hand, claims that Ronald Reagan's strong stand against communism forced Soviet leaders to change. What evidence does each author use to support his or her argument? Whose argument do you find more persuasive? Explain, citing from the texts.

Chapter 4

1. John Garnett admits "it is impossible to prove a connection between the absence of war and the threat made to deter it." He claims, however, that despite this logical difficulty, common sense suggests that mutual deterrence must have had something to do with the fact that the superpowers did not engage in nuclear war. Richard Ned Lebow and Janice Gross Stein argue that the mutual deterrence strategy was too risky, ultimately contributing to the tensions between the two powers that made nuclear war more likely. Both viewpoints seem to agree that the fear of nuclear annihilation had some impact on the decision not to use nuclear weapons. Both also seem to agree that the strategy of mutual deterrence had its risks. What evidence do these authors cite that ultimately brings them to different conclusions? Explain, citing from the texts.

2. Arch Puddington refutes the claims that civil liberties were curtailed during the Cold War, arguing instead that the rights of Americans increased during this period. Puddington cites several examples to support his argument. Which example do you find most persuasive and which the least? Explain.

3. Richard J. Barnet claims that the Soviet Union, at least at the beginning of the Cold War, was not a serious threat. He suggests that had the United States taken Walter Lippmann's diplomatic approach at that time and negotiated with the Soviet Union, the nation might have avoided the costs associated with fighting the Cold War. In light of the evidence provided in his viewpoint, do you think peace with the Soviet Union could have been negotiated? Explain why or why not.

❋ Chronology

1945

February 4–11: Churchill, Stalin, and Roosevelt meet at Yalta.

July: The Soviet Union insists on occupying territories in Eastern Europe at the Potsdam Conference.

August 6 and 9: The United States detonates atomic bombs over Hiroshima and Nagasaki, Japan.

October: U.S. secretary of state James Byrnes and Soviet foreign minister V.B. Molotov meet to begin discussions on the fate of postwar Europe.

1946

March 15: During a speech delivered in Fulton, Missouri, Winston Churchill warns that an "iron curtain" divides the nations of Europe.

June: Congress establishes the Atomic Energy Commission under the Atomic Energy Act of 1946.

October: Soviet-American negotiations over a World War II peace settlement stall.

1947

March: Congress provides aid to Greece and Turkey, implementing the Truman Doctrine.

June: In accordance with the Marshall Plan, the United States offers assistance for the economic recovery of sixteen European nations ravaged by World War II.

1948

February: Supported by the Soviet army, Czech Communists carried out a coup in Prague.

June: Soviet troops block Western access to Berlin. The United States, Britain, and France airlift more than 2 million tons of food and supplies to the city for fifteen months.

1949

April 4: Several Western nations form the North Atlantic Treaty Organization (NATO), a common defense alliance to counterbalance Soviet forces in Eastern Europe.

August 29: The Soviet Union explodes an atomic bomb at Semipalatinsk in Kazakhstan.

September: In alliance with the Soviet Union, Communists under Mao Tse-tung seize control of China from U.S. ally Chiang Kai-shek.

October 7: The German Democratic Republic, also called East Germany, is formed.

1950

February: Senator Joseph McCarthy pursues an anti-Communist crusade, also known as the Red Scare.

June 25: Communist North Korea invades South Korea.

December: Chinese forces check the success of American-led UN forces commanded by General Douglas MacArthur.

1951

April: President Harry S. Truman relieves MacArthur of command for insubordination in pressing for an invasion of China.

1952

November 1: The United States tests its first hydrogen bomb.

1953

July 27: A truce in the Korean War is reached.

August 14: The Soviet Union explodes its first hydrogen bomb.

1954

July: The Geneva Accord partitions Vietnam at the 17th parallel.

September 8: The Southeast Asian Treaty Organization is established.

1955

May 14: The Soviet Union and seven Eastern European countries sign the Warsaw Pact.

June 15: Nationwide civil defense exercises begin in the United States to prepare against nuclear attack.

1956

October 29: British, French, and Israeli troops attack Egypt to take back control of the Suez Canal.

November: Soviet tanks crush a national rebellion against communism in Hungary and thousands flee to the West.

1958

July: U.S. Marines land in Lebanon in support of the local pro-Western government.

November: Khrushchev demands that the United States withdraw troops from West Berlin and declare it a "free city."

1959

February: Fidel Castro seizes control of Cuba, overthrowing right-wing dictator Fulgencio Batista.

September 15: Khrushchev begins his visit to the United States; he is denied access to Disneyland.

1960

May 1: An American U-2 spy plane is shot down over the Soviet Union.

1961

April: A U.S.-sponsored attempt by fifteen hundred Cuban exiles to oust Fidel Castro fails at the Bay of Pigs.

June: Kennedy and Khrushchev meet in Vienna, Austria. Khrushchev calls for support for "wars of national liberation" and demands Western withdrawal from Berlin.

August: East Germany erects the Berlin Wall to stem the flight of its citizens to the West.

1962

The Kennedy administration intensifies its military commitment to South Vietnam.

October: President John F. Kennedy orders a blockade of Cuba to prevent Soviet shipments of nuclear missiles. Khrushchev halts work on launch sites and removes missiles already in Cuba.

1963

> **June 26:** Kennedy visits Berlin and makes the proclamation that he says represents the world of freedom: *"Ich bin ein Berliner."*
> **July 25:** The United States and the Soviet Union ratify a nuclear test ban treaty.

1964

> **August 7:** Congress authorizes expansion of involvement in Vietnam by passing the Gulf of Tonkin Resolution.
> **October 16:** China tests an atomic bomb.

1965

> **July:** President Johnson announces that 150,000 U.S. troops will be dispatched to Vietnam.

1967

> Antiwar rallies are staged in several U.S. cities and in Europe.
> **July:** American troops in South Vietnam number four hundred thousand.

1968

> **February:** The Tet Offensive, a massive Vietcong and North Vietnamese offensive strike against the cities of South Vietnam, reveals the continuing strength of the North Vietnamese army.
> **August 22:** In Prague, Czechoslovakia, Soviet troops crush a revolt against the nation's Communist government.
> **August 26–29:** Police and National Guard troops use tear gas and clubs to keep "hippies" and militants away from the Chicago Democratic Convention.

1969

> **March:** The United States begins heavy bombardment in Cambodia in an effort to eliminate Communist supply routes.
> **June 5:** U.S. secretary of state Henry Kissinger and Xuan Thuy of North Vietnam begin secret meetings to discuss peace.
> **November 3:** President Richard M. Nixon declares his Vietnamization plan.

1970

> **May 4:** Four Kent State University students are killed by National Guardsmen.

June 11: The Soviet Union agrees to continue support of North Vietnam.

1972

February: President Nixon reopens severed ties with China during a ten-day official visit.

April 10: The United States and the Soviet Union sign a biological weapons ban treaty.

May 26: Nixon and Leonid Brezhnev sign the SALT I treaty.

1973

January: The United States and North Vietnam agree on a cease-fire.

March: U.S. troops withdraw from Vietnam.

October: Egypt and Syria attack Israel; Egypt's president Anwar Sadat requests Soviet aid.

1974

July: Congress passes the Jackson-Vanik amendment, tying Soviet-American trade to Soviet willingness to permit Jewish dissidents to leave the Soviet Union.

1975

April 30: The Vietnam War ends as Communist North Vietnamese forces occupy Saigon without resistance.

August 1: The Helsinki Accord is signed.

1978

September: President Jimmy Carter successfully mediates the Egyptian-Israeli Camp David Accords.

1979

January: The United States and China begin to establish diplomatic bonds.

July: Carter and Brezhnev agree to SALT II, which limits each country to twenty-four hundred nuclear arms launchers.

November: The shah of Iran is overthrown; American hostages are seized in Iran.

December 25: The Soviet army invades Afghanistan on Christmas Day.

1980

January 4: The United States stops wheat sales to the Soviet Union.

April 24: An attempt to rescue U.S. hostages in Iran fails.

1981

January 20: The United States released almost $8 billion in Iranian assets and the hostages were freed after 444 days in captivity.

November: President Ronald Reagan signs the secret National Security Decision Directive 17 authorizing the CIA to train and equip the Contras in their war with the Sandinistas in Nicaragua.

1983

March: Reagan proposes the Strategic Defense Initiative (SDI).

August: Soviets shoot down a Korean civilian airliner they claim violated Soviet air space.

1984

January 17: Arms limitation talks between NATO and the Warsaw Pact begin.

March: Reagan visits China, agreeing to sell sophisticated weapons to the Chinese.

1985

February 4: Reagan requests that Congress triple the military budget to support SDI.

March 10: Mikhail Gorbachev launches an economic and political restructuring program called *perestroika*.

April 7: Gorbachev declares a definitive stop to missile deployment in Europe.

1986

October 11: Gorbachev and Reagan meet in Reykjavik, Iceland, and shock the world by agreeing to remove all intermediate-range nuclear missiles from Europe.

November: The Iran-Contra affair is revealed to the American people.

1988

July 16: The Warsaw Pact demands a three-step decrease of conventional weapon units in Europe.

December: Gorbachev renounces the Brezhnev Doctrine, thereby permitting greater freedom to the states of Eastern Europe.

1989

January: Soviet troops withdraw from Afghanistan.

June: Poland becomes independent of Soviet influence, and Lech Walesa and Solidarity come to power.

September: Hungary becomes independent of Soviet influence and the new regime permits East Germans to escape through Hungary to West Germany.

November: The Berlin Wall falls and the East German government opens the country's borders.

December: Communist regimes fall in Czechoslovakia, Bulgaria, and Rumania.

1990

May 30–June 2: Gorbachev and Bush meet in Washington for a four-day summit.

August 31: East and West Germany sign the Unification Treaty.

October 3: Germany is reunited.

1991

July: Hard-line Communists try, but fail, to overthrow Gorbachev and the new Soviet government.

August: The Soviet Union collapses, ending seventy-four years of Soviet communism.

December: The republics of the Soviet Union ally together as the Commonwealth of Independent States.

For Further Research

Lisa A. Baglione, *To Agree or Not to Agree: Leadership, Bargaining, and Arms Control.* Ann Arbor: University of Michigan Press, 1999.

Jian Chen, *Mao's China and the Cold War.* Chapel Hill: University of North Carolina Press, 2001.

Stephen J. Cimbala, *Deterrence and Nuclear Proliferation in the Twenty-first Century.* Westport, CT: Praeger, 2001.

Gerard J. De Groot, *A Noble Cause? America and the Vietnam War.* New York: Longman, 2000.

Lee Edwards, *The Collapse of Communism.* Stanford, CA: Hoover Institution Press, 2000.

Lawrence Freedman, *The Evolution of Nuclear Strategy.* London: Macmillan, 1989.

———, *Kennedy's Wars: Berlin, Cuba, Laos, and Vietnam.* New York: Oxford University Press, 2000.

Norman Friedman, *The Fifty-Year War: Conflict and Strategy in the Cold War.* Annapolis: Naval Institute Press, 2000.

John Lewis Gaddis, *We Now Know: Rethinking Cold War History.* New York: Oxford University Press, 1997.

Robert C. Grogin, *Natural Enemies: The United States and the Soviet Union in the Cold War, 1917–1991.* Lanham, MD: Lexington Books, 2001.

Michael Hickey, *The Korean War: The West Confronts Communism.* Woodstock, NY: Overlook Press, 2000.

Roger Hilsman, *The Cuban Missile Crisis: The Struggle over Policy.* Westport, CT: Praeger, 1996.

Allen Hunter, ed., *Rethinking the Cold War.* Philadelphia: Temple University Press, 1998.

Henry A. Kissinger, *Nuclear Weapons and Foreign Policy*. New York: Harper, 1957.

Walter LaFeber, *America, Russia, and the Cold War, 1945–2000*. Boston: McGraw-Hill, 2002.

Fredrik Logevall, *The Origins of the Vietnam War*. New York: Longman, 2001.

David M. Oshinksy, *A Conspiracy So Immense: The World of Joseph McCarthy*. New York: Macmillan, 1983.

Ronald E. Powaski, *The Cold War: The United States and the Soviet Union, 1917–1991*. New York: Oxford University Press, 1998.

Stanley Sandler, *The Korean War: No Victors, No Vanquished*. Lexington: University Press of Kentucky, 1999.

Orrin Schwab, *Defending the Free World: John F. Kennedy, Lyndon Johnson, and the Vietnam War, 1961–1965*. Westport, CT: Praeger, 1998.

Ezra T. Siff, *Why the Senate Slept: The Gulf of Tonkin Resolution and the Beginning of America's Vietnam War*. Westport, CT: Praeger, 1999.

W.R. Smyser, *From Yalta to Berlin: The Cold War Struggle over Germany*. New York: St. Martin's Press, 1999.

Mary E. Stuckey, *Playing the Game: The Presidential Rhetoric of Ronald Reagan*. Westport, CT: Praeger, 1990.

Richard C. Thornton, *Odd Man Out: Truman, Stalin, Mao, and the Origins of the Korean War*. Washington, DC: Brassey's, 2000.

Ann Tusa, *The Last Division: A History of Berlin, 1945–1989*. Reading, MA: Addison-Wesley, 1997.

John Van Oudenaren, *Détente in Europe: The Soviet Union and the West Since 1953*. Durham, NC: Duke University Press, 1991.

Odd Arne Westad, *Brothers in Arms: The Rise and Fall of the Sino-*

Soviet Alliance, 1945–1963. Stanford, CA: Stanford University Press, 1998.

Odd Arner Westad, ed., *The Fall of Détente: Soviet-American Relations During the Carter Years.* Boston: Scandinavian University Press, 1997.

Mark J. White, *The Cuban Missile Crisis.* Basingstoke, Hampshire, England: Macmillan, 1996.

Websites

A&E Television Networks, The History Channel, www. historychannel.com.

CNN, Cold War: CNN Perspective Series, www.cnn.com/ SPECIALS/coldwar.

Cold War Museum, The Cold War Museum, www.coldwar.org.

✴ Index